WALKING ACROSS

LONDON

Patrick Hamilton

Exploring all sides of the capital in ten
unique and fascinating walks

Capital Travel Books   *Enjoy the walks !*

Patrick Hamilton

First published in 2008 by
Capital Travel Books
PO Box 60167
London SW19 3RX

www.capitaltravelbooks.co.uk
info@capitaltravelbooks.co.uk

Reprinted (with revisions) 2009

ISBN 978-0-9559537-0-5

Cover design by Stuart Dowling, A4 Internet Ltd

Design and page layout by Beth Lucas

Printed by Intype Libra Units 3/4, Elm Grove Industrial Estate, Elm Grove,
Wimbledon, London SW19 4HE

The benefits of exercise

'I awaked as usual heavy, confused, and splenetic. Every morning this is the case with me. Dempster prescribed to me to cut two or three brisk capers round the room, which I did, and found attended with most agreeable effects. It expelled the phlegm from my heart, gave my blood a free circulation, and my spirits a brisk flow; so that I was all at once made happy.'

James Boswell
Boswell's London Journal, Friday 6th May 1763

Acknowledgements

Many people have helped in the preparation of this book, with information, advice, and encouragement. Included amongst these patient, well-informed, and good-natured souls are: all the staff at Camden, Hackney, Lambeth, and Brent archives; Southwark Local History Library; Vestry House Museum; Cuming Museum; Pumphouse Museum; Church Farmhouse Museum, and The Brunel Museum. Also of great help were the Hornsey Historical Society, and the Clapham Society.

For help in all sorts of ways, personal thanks go to: Sarah Anderson, Tony Tucker, Stephen Humphrey, George Shotter, Philip Grant, David Pracy, Barry Hill, Suzy Hamilton, Wendy Hamilton, Alyson Wilson, Ken Gay, Hugh Petrie, Aidan Flood and Ann Hopkins. Thanks also to Rob Julian for making such a splendid job of the maps, to Peter Classey for his entertaining cartoons, to Stuart Dowling for the cover design and to Beth Lucas, heartfelt gratitude for designing the book and turning my plain words into something readable.

To complete the list, many thanks go to Tony Chapman, Moya Birchall and the staff at Intype Libra for their valuable help and expertise in the preparation and printing of the book.

Contents

Foreword   7

Introduction   8

Walk One: *City to City*   10
Bank to Westminster, 4 miles

Walk Two: *Parks and Palaces*   33
St James's Park to Holland Park, 6¼ miles in 2 stages
         St James's Park to Hyde Park Corner 2¼ miles
         Hyde Park Corner to Holland Park 4 miles

Walk Three: *Wilkes and Liberty!*   52
Westminster to Clerkenwell, 8 miles in 2 stages
         Westminster to Waterloo 4 miles
         Waterloo to Clerkenwell 4 miles

Walk Four: *Pleasure Grounds Old and New*   76
Vauxhall to Camden Lock, 8½ miles in 3 stages
         Vauxhall to Trafalgar Square 2 miles
         Trafalgar Square to King's Cross 3 miles
         King's Cross to Camden Lock 3½ miles

Walk Five: *A Taste of Eastern Markets*   97
Walthamstow to Petticoat Lane, 9 miles in 2 stages
         Walthamstow to Hackney 5½ miles
         Hackney to Petticoat Lane 3½ miles

Walk Six: *Secrets of Southwark*   118
London Bridge to Rotherhithe and back, 10½ miles in 2 stages
         London Bridge to Surrey Quays 5½ miles
         Surrey Quays to London Bridge 5 miles

Walk Seven: *The North-West Frontier*   142
Holland Park to Hendon, 12½ miles in 4 stages
     Holland Park to Harlesden 3½ miles
     Harlesden to Willesden Green 2¼ miles
     Willesden Green to Neasden 3 miles
     Neasden to Hendon 3¾ miles

Walk Eight: *Peaks and Troughs*   166
Wood Green to Notting Hill, 13 miles in 4 stages
     Wood Green to Highgate Village 4 miles
     Highgate Village to Chalk Farm 3 miles
     Chalk Farm to Little Venice 3 miles
     Little Venice to Notting Hill 3 miles

Walk Nine: *Village Life*   200
Deptford to Brixton, 14 miles in 3 stages
     Deptford to Peckham Rye 5½ miles
     Peckham Rye to Clapham 6 miles
     Clapham to Brixton 2½ miles

Walk Ten: *Watermen's Woe*   228
Hammersmith to Tower Hill, 15 miles in 4 stages
     Hammersmith to Wandsworth 4 miles
     Wandsworth to Pimlico 4½ miles
     Pimlico to Blackfriars 3½ miles
     Blackfriars to Tower Hill 3 miles

Contacts   257

Bibliography   259

Index   261

Foreword

Discovery and walking are two of life's pleasures, and when combined with London, a place of huge variety and hidden gems, the combination becomes irresistible.

This collection of walks is useful for Londoners and non-Londoners alike. The walks offer close-up views of well-known iconic buildings and spaces and views, plus little known ancient streets and corners.

Also, as someone who once set off on a 14-mile country walk assuming there'd be a café *somewhere* on the way (there wasn't), I particularly appreciate the refreshments advice.

An important part of my work as an elected politician has been about encouraging walking for the health of individual walkers, for the health of air quality for all Londoners and to soften London's impact on the planet.

Here is a book to tempt us all to walk for fun, for exercise, or even to arrive somewhere.

Cllr Jenny Jones
Green Party Member of the London Assembly

Introduction

Exploring the capital on foot, with this book to guide you, is an excellent way to delve deeply under London's skin, and find out what makes this city so fascinating. *Walking Across London* is packed with interest, the emphasis being on scenic, historical, and architectural highlights. To get your feet twitching, a taster of the wealth of variety on offer includes such delights as travelling over, under, or across most of London's Thames bridges; visiting peaceful canal towpaths and bustling markets; straying off the beaten tourist track to investigate some historic 'villages' such as Rotherhithe, Walthamstow, or Highgate; or just marvelling at the splendid views to be had from Alexandra Palace, Parliament Hill, or Westminster Bridge.

These, and many other pleasures, will keep you entertained in this collection of ten walks, all but one divided into separate, shorter stages. Plentiful public transport on virtually all the routes means that you can go as far as the mood takes you; in fact several of the walks link up to form east-west, or north-south journeys of epic proportions.

So just choose your route, put on your most comfortable walking shoes, and let *Walking Across London* be your companion.

Things you need to know

Each walk is described in stages, with details of:

> Distance
> Approximately how much time to allow, at a leisurely pace
> En-route or nearby toilets, cafés, and pubs
> The terrain
> Public transport details, with the relevant fare zones
> The best time to do the walk

Tickets and fares

Check the fare zones that you will be travelling in; it's cheaper if you don't need Zone 1, but remember that if you are travelling through this zone you will need a ticket that covers it. Oyster cards offer the cheapest fares for Tube, Docklands Light Rail (DLR), bus, and tram, but have limited use on National Rail routes. If your journey involves rail travel, a Travelcard, available for peak or off-peak, will probably be your best choice. These cards can be purchased at station ticket offices, some newsagents, and in the case of Oyster cards, by phone on 0845 330 9876, or online at tfl. gov.uk/oyster. Freedom Passes for the over 60s issued by the London boroughs will provide free travel to and from all the walks. Transport for London (TfL) provides information for bus, Tube, trams, DLR, and local rail services on 020 7222 1234 or tfl.gov.uk

Helpful hints

If you find the miles are telling on you, or the weather is awful, or for any other reason you have had enough, there are plenty of intermediate staging posts. Train and Tube stations on or near the walk are listed, and there are usually bus stops not too far away. All the walks begin and end at a station or bus stop, and are within fare zones 1–4.

Re-fuelling stops for food and drink are important to maintain your energy, so do check the 'Refreshments' section for each stage. Most of the routes offer somewhere pleasant to picnic, very often in delightful surroundings, but whatever your choice, a bit of planning before you set out is a good idea.

Most parks and gardens, and even some paths, are closed at night, so don't be too ambitious with your mileage, especially in the winter months. There's always another day to do that last bit. Occasionally a road or path may be closed for any number of reasons, so it is important to have a street atlas to hand, which you can also refer to along the way to confirm the route. All the walks can be enjoyed on any day of the week, but some facilities are restricted on Sundays, including public transport. The various markets that are mentioned are usually thronging at weekends, which add plenty of entertainment but also a lot of time to your schedule. Many buildings of note, old and new, that are normally out of bounds are open to the public on the annual Open House Weekend in September.

The pace of change in London is quite startling. New buildings appear, while others disappear; names, particularly of pubs, often follow the fashion of the day; and new developments can alter a whole neighbourhood. The walks in this book were devised and written between 2006 and 2008, and have all been updated before publication, but details of any inaccuracies, or any comments about the walks, would be welcome.

1 City to City

Bank to Westminster

Ringed with majestic buildings, the junction simply known as 'Bank' provides a splendid departure point for this tour of a historic corner of the City of London, where mingled amongst the 'Wren churches' built shortly after the Great Fire of London in 1666 is a cluster of age-old livery halls of the long-established trade guilds. The route then heads south, through half-forgotten Dickensian back-streets, until the familiar landmarks of Big Ben and the Houses of Parliament herald your arrival in the City of Westminster, where you will see some of London's most dramatic and awe-inspiring architecture.

Distance 4 miles. Intermediate distances: Bankside 1 mile, Blackfriars Road 2 miles, Westminster Bridge 3 miles.

Time 3 hours.

Terrain Paved and reasonably level, some cobblestones.

Refreshments A scattering of cafés and pubs around Bank, particularly in Cannon Street and Watling Street/Bow Lane. This is true of Southwark also, until you reach The Cut and Lower Marsh, which provide plenty of choice. Around St James's Park station at the end of the walk there are two or three cafés and pubs.

Toilets Bank station, Suffolk Lane near Cannon Street station, Waterloo station, Bridge Street Westminster.

Transport Fare zone 1. Bank (DLR, Tube, bus), Mansion House (Tube, bus), Cannon Street (train, Tube, bus), Southwark (Tube, bus), Waterloo and Waterloo East (train, Tube, bus), Westminster (Tube, bus), St James's Park (Tube).

Best time to do the walk Monday to Friday, when you will find the shops, cafés, pubs, and several of the churches open.

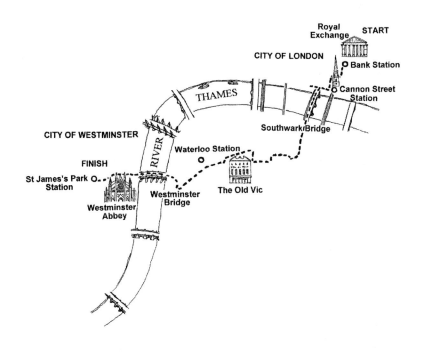

Royal Exchange
START
CITY OF LONDON
○ Bank Station
Cannon Street Station
THAMES
CITY OF WESTMINSTER
Southwark Bridge
RIVER
Waterloo Station
FINISH
○
St James's Park Station ○
The Old Vic
Westminster Bridge
Westminster Abbey

Right: The Royal Exchange, completed in 1844, marks the start of the City to City walk

The Bank of England owes its existence to the need to raise money for war against France in the 17th century. A Scotsman, William Paterson, proposed a scheme whereby loans to the State were repaid by taxes on goods, with the bank also offering deposit and current accounts to the public. Sir John Houblon, descendant of a French Protestant refugee, became the first governor in 1694. You'll see his bewigged features on a modern-day £50 note.

Above: a gilded grasshopper tops the Royal Exchange

Start at Bank station (Northern, Central, District, and Circle lines, DLR, Waterloo and City line). Take exit 3 for Royal Exchange (there are toilets by this exit).

This is the third Royal Exchange on this site, the previous two having succumbed to fire. Sir Thomas Gresham, banker and goldsmith, laid the foundation stone of the first building in 1566, and his crest, a grasshopper, still adorns the rear elevation. Queen Elizabeth I performed the official opening in 1571, apparently spending some time in the 'pawn', a high-class shopping arcade on the first floor, and it was she who christened the building the 'Royal Exchange'. Its purpose was to provide a 'bourse' or trading place for merchants, a role fulfilled for over 300 years, by which time many of the occupants, great financial institutions such as the Stock Exchange and Lloyds, needed their own, larger, premises. The building you see today, faced with massive Corinthian columns, contains in its sumptuous interior shops and coffee houses much the same as its predecessor and was opened by a young Queen Victoria in 1844.

Facing the Royal Exchange, go right, then left along Cornhill for 100 yards, where a tall, blue hand-pump marks the spot where you turn left into Royal Exchange Buildings.

Right: The Bank
of England was
heightened and
rebuilt by Sir Herbert
Baker between
the wars but still
retains the original
impenetrable
outer walls

Right: The Bank of England was heightened and rebuilt by Sir Herbert Baker between the wars but still retains the original impenetrable outer walls

High above, if you crane your neck, you will see a statue of Sir Thomas Gresham under his trademark grasshopper, which gleams gold atop the clock tower. The other statues here are of George Peabody, American philanthropist and social housing pioneer, comfortably seated in his armchair, and Paul Julius Reuter, of news agency fame.

Turn left to complete a circuit of the exterior of the building and arrive at your starting point, then with your back to the Royal Exchange glance across to your right, to the Bank of England, the 'Old Lady of Threadneedle Street'.

Since the establishment of a purpose-built home for the bank in 1734 there has been much extending and rebuilding, mostly in keeping with Sir John Soane's 18th-century remodelling of this 3 acre site. The bluff surrounding walls are his creation. Although it has always operated as the national bank, it was not in fact nationalized until 1946.

Gold bars, bank note designs, old coins and documents, and inter-active features are on display at the excellent

Bank of England Museum in Bartholomew Lane, which is open Monday to Friday 10.00-17.00 (except Bank Holidays, understandably), admission free.

A fascinating sample of the City of London's long history is contained in the names of the streets that converge at Bank. Commerce and trade are represented, first at Poultry, part of the great 'cheap', or market, which is now Cheapside; Lombard Street, where money-lenders from the Lombardy region of Italy settled in the 13th century; Threadneedle Street, referred to by John Stow in his 'Survey of London' in 1598 as Three Needle Street, three needles being the arms of the Needlemaker's Company; and Cornhill, named either for a corn market here, or an important City family called Cornhell.

Below: Bank street scene

In deference to royalty there is Prince's Street, King William Street, and Queen Victoria Street, the last two not appearing until the 19th century, having been sliced through the tangle of lanes, courts, and alleys to relieve traffic congestion on the roads to London Bridge and

Left: Surveying the busy scene at Bank, the Duke of Wellington is backed by the Royal Exchange

Aldgate. Cannon Street, now a major thoroughfare, at that time was just a narrow lane. Heading downhill towards the Thames is the street named Walbrook, where centuries ago a stream flowed. This long-lost watercourse rose in the marshy area of Moorfields, just outside the northern part of the City wall, but was mostly covered over by the 15th century.

Walk towards the statue of the Duke of Wellington, seated on his horse. Bear left across Cornhill, at the traffic lights, to Lombard Street, where you turn left for 50 yards to the church of St Mary Woolnoth.

St Mary Woolnoth is the only City church of the six London churches designed by Nicholas Hawksmoor. His best-known work outside the City is probably the recently-restored Christ Church, Spitalfields. St Mary Woolnoth was completed in 1727, and then modified by William Butterfield in 1875–76, when the seating galleries were removed, leaving just their fronts set against the walls. Although the exterior is somewhat austere, the richness of the interior is quite dazzling, with clusters of fluted columns supporting a high, naturally-lit ceiling. Just below this is a cheerful trio of cherubs next to a royal coat of arms. More cherubs, this time gilded, look down from above the altar, while the inlaid pulpit with its high tester competes for your attention. When the City and South London Railway built Bank station in the 1890s the church was threatened with demolition, but the final outcome involved removal of old burials from the crypt, which ended up as part of the station's booking hall.

Above: The Mansion House

After visiting the church turn back towards the traffic lights and go left across Lombard Street, then turn right for a few yards to the Mansion House.

The Mansion House is the Lord Mayor of London's official residence. Before the completion of this building in 1753, when Sir Crisp Gascoigne became

15

the first Lord Mayor to move in, this important figure would entertain guests in his own house, or in a hired house. Previously the site was occupied by the centuries-old Stocks Market, so named because the City stocks stood here, into which wrongdoers would be placed as punishment, unable to protect themselves from being pelted with rotten fruit or worse. Nearby stood the church of St Mary Woolchurch Haw, where at one time a beam was placed, in the churchyard, for the weighing of wool.

Above: No 1 Poultry is quite unique amongst the surrounding grandeur

George Dance the Elder designed the Mansion House, the grandest part of which is the State Banqueting Room, known as the Egyptian Hall. Resplendent with Corinthian columns, barrel ceiling, and 23 carat gold-leaf decoration, it accommodates nearly 400 guests. When first built it was topped by another storey, one part of which, dubbed 'Noah's Ark', was removed by George Dance the Younger in 1795. The foundations are built on wooden piles to solve the problem of the proximity of the Walbrook stream and its gravelly flood-plain.

Open House weekend in September provides an opportunity to view the interior, if you are fortunate enough to be allotted tickets, which must be pre-booked.

Pass the Mansion House and pause on the corner of Walbrook.

Look towards Queen Victoria Street, where facing you is the bold outline of No 1 Poultry. With its central clock tower, beige and terra cotta stripes, and higgledy-piggledy arrangement, it presents a marked contrast to its near neighbours. Completed in 1998, it was designed by Stirling and Wilford, with a landscaped terrace, office space, a central open area, and shops, with access to Bank station. Further to the right is the former Midland Bank headquarters, built 1924–39, which was designed by Sir Edwin Lutyens.

Right: Filled with
natural light, the
interior of St Stephen
Walbrook is topped
with a 50-ton dome,
supported on slender
corner columns

Right: Filled with natural light, the interior of St Stephen Walbrook is topped with a 50-ton dome, supported on slender corner columns

Turn left into Walbrook, passing Wren's St Stephen Walbrook Church.

Sir Christopher Wren, the architect of this church which was built 1672–79 beside the covered-over Walbrook stream, planned the dome with its green copper cladding and richly decorated interior before he tackled the world-famous dome of St Paul's. Perhaps he used it as a prototype. The geometric perfection of St Stephen's interior, with squares, circles, and semicircles of dome and ceiling supported on unobtrusive corner columns, provides a surprisingly open central space. Much of the woodwork has survived from Wren's time, and although the Victorians added stained glass, daylight now shines through clear windows, as it would originally have done, after wartime blast damage was made good.

The Samaritans came into being in this church in 1953, through the efforts of the Rector, Chad Varah, and the telephone on which the first call was made from the church vestry is mounted on a plinth inside. Henry Moore carved the circular altar, which was placed in the centre of the church in the 1980s restoration.

Left: The entrance to Skinners' Hall, one of Dowgate Hill's age-old livery halls

At Cannon Street (Tube and rail stations here), cross at the lights and continue downhill, now on Dowgate Hill (if you wish to see the London Stone, said to be London's oldest outdoor relic, turn left along Cannon Street for 100 yards, where you will find it tucked into the wall of a building on the left, just beyond Salter's Hall Court).

Immediately on your right in Dowgate Hill are three livery halls in quick succession; the Tallow Chandlers', Skinners', and Dyers'. These halls, along with more than 30 others, are the headquarters of the various age-old trade guilds, which are still very much alive today, but largely as charitable institutions. They have always been governed by strict rules and ancient traditions, and yet there are still new entrants, the Company of Information Technologists becoming the 100th City of London livery company when they were granted their charter in 1992.

The great rivalry for the order of precedence amongst the companies was finally settled in 1515 with the Mercers at number one, followed by Grocers, Drapers, Fishmongers, and Goldsmiths. However, the Merchant Taylors and Skinners were unable to agree on places 6 and 7, which it was decided they would occupy on alternate years, hence the phrase 'at sixes and sevens'.

The companies whose three halls you now pass all have long and eventful histories, which include these very brief snippets of past interest:

The Tallow Chandlers have occupied this site since 1476, and used to have power of search in and around the City for poor quality, or 'naughty', tallow, candles, soap, butter, oil, vinegar, and hops.

The Skinners were granted their first charter in the reign of Edward III, in 1327. The present hall dates from 1669, with a new front added in 1791.

The Dyers were first mentioned as a guild in 1188. They are responsible for swans on the Thames, together with the Vintners' Company and the Crown.

Take the next right turn into College Street. Pass the Innholders' Hall on the left, then the church of St Michael Paternoster Royal on the right.

Included in the history of the Innholders is a reference to W J Chaplin, at one time a member of this company, who distinguished himself by being the landlord of the White Horse, Fetter Lane; the Spread Eagle and Cross Keys in Gracechurch Street; the Swan with Two Necks in Lad Lane; and the Spread Eagle West-End coaching office in Regent Circus. In addition to the inns, at one time he owned 68 coaches. He was Master of the Company from 1854–55, as well as being MP for Salisbury.

St Michael's name is interesting, like so many City church names; 'Paternoster' refers to the rosaries that were made nearby, and 'Royal' is a corruption of 'Le Reole', a French wine-making town whose name was adopted for this area of wine-importing wharves. This was Dick Whittington's church, in which he worshipped and in which he was buried in 1423. Four times Lord Mayor of London, he became a wealthy mercer, a dealer in fine cloth, and gave generously to many good causes. St Michael's was rebuilt by Wren after the Great Fire of 1666, but suffered greatly in the last war; in the 1960s restoration of the church new woodwork and dramatic stained glass windows were installed. The Mission to Seafarers, 'caring for seafarers around the world' has its headquarters here.

Above: Parish boundary markers, College Street

Cross Queen Street to maintain your direction along cobbled Skinner's Lane for 75 yards to 'Wren's Lantern', the church of St James, Garlickhythe.

Scallop shells, which can be seen throughout the church, were the emblem of St James of Compostella, who was martyred in Spain in the year 44 AD. The church was dedicated to St James in the 14th century, and named after a nearby hythe, or jetty, where garlic would have been imported.

Following the Great Fire of London, £5,357 had to be paid for a new church, designed by Wren, which opened its doors in 1682. In common with so many other London churches, pale, finely-textured Portland stone was specified for the building, arriving by sea from Dorset. The steeple is particularly complex and beautiful, with urns, a 3-stage lantern, and ascending tiers of decorative stone. The ornate clock, topped by a carving of St James, is actually a convincing 1980s replica.

In World War II, the church had a lucky escape when a 500 lb bomb scored a direct hit on the south-east corner, but did not explode. However in 1991 a tower crane on a nearby building site toppled over and crashed through the wall, smashing the rose window, chandelier, and pews. The church is now fully restored, and with the high ceiling, decorated with blue sky and a few clouds, and so much light admitted by the clear glass windows, the title of 'Wren's Lantern' is fully justified.

Retrace your steps 75 yards back to Queen Street, turn right and cross Lower Thames Street at traffic lights, and keep ahead towards Southwark Bridge.

Below: A bountiful figure at Vintners Place

Adjacent to your crossing of Lower Thames Street is Vintners' Hall, in the City ward known as Vintry. The Vintners' Company has been established on or near this site since the 13th century, and still maintains ancient customs such as the annual Swan Voyage, or 'Swan Upping', keeping tabs on the birds along the Thames' upper reaches. You may have noticed the life-size statue of the Barge Master and Swan Marker next to St James's Church. A good story from the Vintners' illustrious history concerns Henry Picard, Vintner and Lord Mayor 1356–57, who was said to have entertained at his house five kings; of England, Scotland, France, Denmark, and Cyprus, giving rise to the Vintners' toast of five cheers.

Cross Southwark Bridge to arrive in the district known as Bankside.

As you stride across the surging Thames, there is much of interest to see; to your right, upstream, are

Tate Modern, the Globe Theatre, and the Millennium Bridge, while downstream the vista is quite different; the tower and turrets of Southwark Cathedral, trains trundling in and out of Cannon Street station, and the unmistakeable outline of Tower Bridge.

Southwark Bridge originally opened as a toll bridge in 1819. Known at that time as the Iron Bridge, its central arch, at 240 ft, was the largest casting ever made, and the total weight of all the ironwork was a colossal 5780 tons. This massive structure, designed by John Rennie, lasted for a century before being replaced by the present bridge in 1921. It was, and still is, the least-used of London's bridges; in the days of trams only one route crossed it, and nowadays it is host to just one bus route.

Carry on straight ahead on Southwark Bridge Road, crossing Southwark Street and then Union Street.

At Union Street the curiously-named Flat Iron Square is home to the Island Café, around which is a selection of modest commercial buildings, many dating from the 1800s, which are typical of this mixed area. On the right is the stylish, imposing former St Saviour's Public Library, while 50 yards further on is Playhouse Court, a quaint courtyard that until recently contained the entrance to the Southwark Playhouse.

Press on around the right-hand curve of Southwark Bridge Road, where, after crossing Doyce Street, you will arrive in front of The Borough Welsh Congregational Chapel.

Charles Dickens knew this area well, having lodged in nearby Lant Street while his father spent three months in the Marshalsea Debtor's Prison. The youthful Dickens had been found a job in a blacking factory at Hungerford Stairs, and his immediate neighbourhood would have provided a rich source of material for the novels that would one day spring from his fertile mind.

The unwholesome district of the Mint was right on his doorstep, and Borough High Street's inns and taverns were just a stone's throw away.

The elder Dickenses apparently lived in reasonable comfort in the Marshalsea. They were joined at mealtimes by their son, who in later years featured the prison as birthplace and home of Amy, in 'Little Dorrit'. A local school and pub still bear the name of Charles Dickens, and his heroes are remembered locally in Pickwick, Weller, Quilp, Dorrit, and Copperfield Streets. You can be forgiven for thinking you have stepped back 150 years amongst the rustic surroundings in this corner of old Southwark.

The London Fire Brigade Museum and Training Centre is 100 yards ahead, whereas your route turns right. If you wish to visit the museum, a phone call is necessary to book a tour, which takes place at 10:30 and 14:00, Monday-Friday.

Below: You must behave yourself in Great Guildford Street

Take the next right into Great Guildford Street (note the command, painted on the right-hand wall a few yards along, to 'commit no nuisance'), and **then turn immediately left to follow Copperfield Street,** with a perfect picnic spot at All Hallows Church Gardens on your right. To visit the Charles Dickens pub take the second right, Risborough Street, but for the main walk carry on along Copperfield Street, at the end of which turn left into Great Suffolk Street (there are one or two cafés and a pub, to your right). Continue for 90 yards **then turn right into Pocock Street.** Follow this quiet back road, passing The Draper's Almshouses. At the end of Pocock Street **turn right to follow Blackfriars Road** to the junction with Union Street and The Cut.

It would be hard to imagine a greater contrast of architectural styles than is evident here in Blackfriars Road. At number 176 stands an example of grandiose Edwardian importance embodied in the Sons of

Temperance Friendly Society's HQ, while across the road, on the left, there is a dose of well-proportioned late 18th-century dwellings, particularly numbers 81–86. Opposite ultra-modern Southwark station, on the corner of Union Street, is Palestra at 197 Blackfriars Road. This glass goliath has a cladding of coloured panels, which look good in daylight, but do not really show up after darkness falls; then the building gives a good impression of a cruise liner that has seriously lost its way. Palestra was designed by Alsop Architects, has 300,000 sq ft of floor space, and opened in 2006.

Under the adjacent railway bridge you can spy the bold wording that announces Blackfriars station. This short-lived stop on the Charing Cross Railway opened in 1864 and closed five years later on the completion of Waterloo East station.

Turn left to follow The Cut. Cross to the right-hand pavement and continue to Waterloo Road, which you cross to **carry on along Baylis Road.**

Walking along The Cut, you will have passed the Young Vic and Old Vic theatres, whose patrons are well-fed by the wide choice of local restaurants. The Young Vic, which opened in 1970, concentrates on giving fledgling young directors a chance, staging experimental productions. It has recently benefited from a £12.5m rebuilding project.

The Old Vic started life in 1818 as the Royal Coburg Theatre, being renamed the Royal Victoria, for the future Queen, in 1833. Music Hall was the staple entertainment, enjoyed by a boisterous and enthusiastic audience. Later, under the management of Miss Emma Cons, the performances took on a more genteel tone, and on her death in 1912 her niece, Lilian Baylis, took over the reins. As well as concentrating more on Shakespeare, she found time to re-open Sadler's Wells Theatre in Islington, with the emphasis on ballet. The new National Theatre was based here from 1963 until acquiring its own home on the South Bank in 1976. Known as 'the actor's theatre', the list of great names that have performed here reads like a Who's Who of the acting profession.

Continue on Baylis Road (which incidentally is named after Lilian Baylis), cross Spur Road and keep ahead along Lower Marsh.

Lower Marsh, part of Lambeth Marsh which was drained and built on in the 19th century, contains several independent shops, including a transport bookshop, an establishment that offers 20th-century vintage clothing and memorabilia, and a scattering of stalls that are the last vestiges of a mile-long market that flourished in the 1800s.

In Westminster Bridge Road, number 121 (85 yards to the left) can be forgiven for having a rather sepulchral air about it; it used to be the London Necropolis station, where from 1902 until 1941 special trains took London's overflow of burials to be interred at a huge, specially-reserved cemetery at Brookwood, Surrey. The service had been operating from a nearby site since 1854, and offered mourners of different means segregated carriages, for the well-off or the poor, and separate areas of burial for Anglican or non-conformist.

At the end of Lower Marsh **cross Westminster Bridge Road and bear right,** through a tunnel, along Upper Marsh. Follow this road to its end at Royal Street; **turn right, then cross Lambeth Palace Road at pedestrian lights towards St Thomas's Hospital. Turn right to continue past the hospital entrance** and the Florence Nightingale Museum.

St Thomas's is one of London's very oldest hospitals, having been founded as part of the Priory of St Mary Overie, near London Bridge, in the 12th century. It was run by the Augustinians, whose monks and nuns were known for helping the homeless, people in need, and the poor. A ferocious fire reduced the hospital to ashes in 1212, but within three years it had been rebuilt on the eastern side of London Bridge. Henry VIII closed the hospital in 1540, but it was resurrected by his son Edward VI in 1552. Three centuries later, construction of the railway from Charing Cross caused the complete rebuilding of St Thomas's on its present site, by 1871. Several of these Victorian buildings can still be seen at the back of the hospital, by the river.

Surprisingly, there is still a remnant of St Thomas's near London Bridge; the Old Operating Theatre and Herb Garret, which remained sealed and forgotten for nearly a century until being rediscovered in 1956.

Left: Made of Coade stone, the South Bank Lion, painted red, adorned the now-demolished Red Lion Brewery before being saved and installed here

The Florence Nightingale Museum recalls 'The Lady of the Lamp', hero of the Crimean War, and pioneer of nurse training. Opening hours are Monday-Friday 10.00-17.00 (last admission 16.00), Saturday, Sunday, and Bank Holiday Mondays 10.00-16.30 (last admission 15.30).

Press on past the hospital, as your route swings round to the left to cross Westminster Bridge.

Over to your right is the Edwardian grandeur of County Hall, former home of the London County Council (LCC), which became the Greater London Council (GLC) in 1965. The foundation stone was laid by King George V in 1912, with the outbreak of war delaying completion until ten years later; several extensions and additions were finally completed by 1963. In 1986 the Prime Minister, Margaret Thatcher, abolished the GLC (although it has now reappeared in a new guise further down-river at City Hall), and County Hall now houses the London Aquarium, Dali Universe, two hotels, cafés and toilets. The ever-popular London Eye is on the riverbank here, next to County Hall.

Keeping a watchful eye on the passers-by is the rather sad countenance of the South Bank Lion, which used to live atop the nearby Red Lion Brewery. When the brewery was demolished the lion, partly through the interest of King George VI, was saved and placed in this commanding position. It is made of Coade stone, an artificial, weatherproof stone used for all sorts of statuary and figures, of which there are many examples dotted around the capital. Made locally in a factory run by Mrs Eleanor Coade, the secret of this hard-wearing material was lost when the firm closed in 1840.

Westminster Bridge's handsome outlines were planned by the architect, Thomas Page, to harmonise with the Houses of Parliament. The bridge opened in 1862, replacing an earlier bridge of 1750, at that time the only alternative crossing to London Bridge. Note the crests set into the parapet, amongst which are those of Queen Victoria, Edward Prince of Wales, and Albert, Prince Consort.

As you cross the bridge, look right to see the statue of Boadicea and her two daughters in their chariot, in headlong, windswept advance on Roman London, to wreak revenge for the wrongs against her Iceni tribe. The work is by Thomas Thornycroft, 1902.

Left: Boadicea seems to have very little control over her horses as they gallop onto Westminster Bridge

The large building on the adjacent corner, with those tall chimneys, is Portcullis House, which provides offices for Members of Parliament. Reckoned to be bomb-proof, it is supported on just six columns on top of Westminster station ticket hall. It was built in 2001.

Press on past the clock tower of Big Ben (there are toilets in the subway here), to the junction with Parliament Square.

On this corner history was made that would change traffic flows across the globe for ever; John Peake Knight installed his new invention, the world's first traffic lights, here in 1868.

To the right of the square, on the corner of Parliament

Street, the large, important-looking turreted building goes by the unflattering nickname of 'GOGGS'; Government Offices Great George Street. Housed within are offices of the Treasury, Revenue & Customs, and other Government departments. It was built 1903-15.

Turn left into Parliament Square, passing the heavily-guarded entrance to the Houses of Parliament.

The Houses of Parliament, Lords and Commons, have been collectively known as The Palace of Westminster since Edward the Confessor built a small palace here in the 11th century so that he could oversee the rebuilding of Westminster Abbey. Even kings needed help and advice, and over the centuries, meetings between kings and their advisors came to be known as a 'parlement', or a talking. Eventually royalty moved away to new palaces, and Westminster Hall, the central part of the Palace of Westminster which William II had built around 1097, became a court of law, a forerunner of the law-making assembly that we have today.

This ancient hall thankfully survived a disastrous fire in 1834 which destroyed virtually all the old palace. The new buildings that emerged, designed by Sir Charles Barry, were given their Gothic embellishments by his collaborator, Augustus Welby Pugin. Between them they produced the most spectacular, decorative, and dramatic building.

Cross right at pedestrian lights to follow the left-hand side of the square to St Margaret's Church (displaying blue sundials, instead of the usual clock faces, on the tower) and Westminster Abbey.

St Margaret's, Parliament's 'parish church', is a part of Westminster Abbey, and not in the Diocese of London. Famous people who were married here include Samuel Pepys in 1655, John Milton in 1656 (there is a stained glass 'Milton Window' in the church), and Winston Churchill in 1908.

Sir Walter Raleigh's body was brought here to be buried after his execution for treason in 1618, and on the outside of the east wall the bust of another famous figure in history, King Charles I, faces the statue of Oliver Cromwell, a signatory to the King's death warrant, standing outside Westminster Hall. The church contains a rich assortment of memorials going back to the 16th century, and much beautiful stained glass, some of it modern.

Left: Guarded by a watchful lion, the glum figure of Oliver Cromwell stands outside Westminster Hall

Westminster Abbey has been the crowning place of kings and queens since William the Conqueror claimed the throne here on Christmas Day 1066. The scene as you enter is enough to stop you in your tracks; you are immediately surrounded by exquisitely carved marble figures, some larger than life, drawing your eye to the impossibly high, intricately decorated ceiling. As you tour round the separate parts of the abbey, each new discovery is awe-inspiring; The Coronation Chair; the tomb of Elizabeth I and her sister Mary; the Lady Chapel, which is absolutely covered in the richest carving and alive with colour and light; and the shrine of St Edward the Confessor. On a lighter note, many famous writers and poets are commemorated in Poet's Corner, including Dr Samuel Johnson, Robert Browning, and Charles Dickens. Two unique features worth looking out for elsewhere in the abbey

Right: Designed by Nicholas Hawksmoor, the West Towers of Westminster Abbey were built 1735-45

are a statue of St Matthew wearing spectacles; and England's oldest door, of about 1050. Opening times of Westminster Abbey vary so do check first, using the contact information listed, if you intend to visit.

From the abbey, **cross at the lights to Little George Street**, then turn left along Broad Sanctuary, passing the Queen Elizabeth II Conference Centre (built in 1986), and heading for dome-topped Methodist Central Hall. There are toilets on the corner of Storey's Gate.

As you crossed from the abbey you may have noticed the Gothic-style building facing Parliament Square; built of Portland stone and completed in 1913, this used to be the Middlesex Guildhall, but is soon to be reincarnated as the United Kingdom Supreme Court.

The Methodist Central Hall is quite a sight; swags, columns, angels, animals, and all sorts of embellishments, the whole lot supported by an unseen reinforced concrete frame. Opened in 1912, it was designed by Lanchester and Rickards, who were also responsible for Deptford Town Hall (see Walk Nine).

Cross Storey's Gate, passing the Methodist Central Hall on your right, to **follow Tothill Street to arrive at St James's Park station**. The 'City to City' walk ends here, with a couple of cafés and a choice of pubs to tempt you in for a **celebratory drink,** well-earned after walking all that way from another City.

2 Parks and Palaces

St James's Park to Holland Park in two stages

This walk is a glorious foray into some of the most delightful parkland scenery that the capital has to offer, attended by the nation's best-loved royal palaces. From the verdant environs of St James's Park the walk slips through Green Park, then onwards through Hyde Park to the Serpentine. Kensington Gardens, home to the famous Peter Pan statue, leads you to Kensington Palace, from where the route travels swiftly to a park with a unique appeal to young and old; Holland Park. Although all the parks welcome visitors, remember some of them will close as early as 16:15 in winter, but overall you shouldn't have any problems with access between 07:30 and dusk.

Stage One: St James's Park to Hyde Park Corner

Distance 2¼ miles. Intermediate distance: St James's Palace 1 mile.

Time 1½ -2 hours.

Terrain Tarmac and paved paths with one short slope; one flight of steps, easily avoided.

Refreshments Two or three cafés and pubs around St James's Park station at the start, with several kiosks, and one café, along the way.

Toilets St James's Park and Hyde Park Corner.

Transport Fare zone 1. St James's Park (Tube), Westminster (Tube, bus), Green Park (Tube, bus), Hyde Park Corner (Tube, bus).

Best time to do the walk On a bright day, to enjoy the scenery and wildlife.

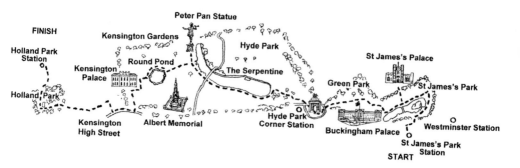

FINISH

Holland Park
Station

Holland Park

Peter Pan Statue

Kensington Gardens

Round Pond

Kensington
Palace

Kensington
High Street

Albert Memorial

Hyde Park

The Serpentine

Hyde Park
Corner Station

Green Park

St James's Palace

St James's Park

Buckingham Palace

St James's Park
Station

START

Westminster Station

Left: Kensington
Gardens has the statue
of Physical Energy as
a powerful focal point

The building from whose depths you emerge at St James's Park station is 55 Broadway, SW1, the headquarters of London Underground. It was designed by Charles Holden, the architect responsible for many of the simple but pleasing 1920s and 30s Tube stations that thousands pass through every day without a second glance. This grand structure dates from 1929, and exhibits exterior sculptures by Jacob Epstein, Henry Moore, and others.

Below: Original features such as these richly carved door hoods add to the 18th- century charm of Queen Anne's Gate

Start at St James's Park station (District and Circle lines). Take the exit for Broadway, then use the zebra crossing at Petty France to go ahead along Queen Anne's Gate. Follow this street as it bears round to the right.

Three hundred years ago this was a fashionable address, and the same can still be said today. A profusion of blue plaques bear witness to the great names that have resided here, in the company of a statue of Queen Anne, which adorns a wall adjacent to number 15. She looks quite sober here, but apparently liked a little tipple, earning her the soubriquet of 'Brandy Nan'. The first part of the street, which used to be Queen Square, contains terraces dating from around 1704, with exceptional carved decoration on the door hoods, and grotesque faces peering at you from the brickwork. A little later in construction, but still handsome, the street's second 'leg' displays styles of house-building from the 1770s to the days of Queen Victoria.

At the T-junction with Dartmouth Street, with the Two Chairmen pub opposite, turn left and after 30 yards descend Cockpit Steps, on the left. To avoid this, retrace your walk to turn right through Queen Anne's Gate, then right to arrive at the foot of the steps.

Cockpit Steps recalls the days of cock-fighting, when in the 18th century a cock-pit existed here, one of half-a-dozen in London. These are now alive in street names only; Cockpit Yard and Cockspur Street, where spurs could be bought for fighting-cocks; and Cock Hill, where the birds were bred. This age-old entertainment, which was depicted by such famous artists as Thomas Rowlandson, became illegal in 1849.

You emerge from the steps onto Birdcage Walk. **Cross directly to a path heading diagonally right across a corner of St James's Park.** Keep ahead at a crossing path, then bear left, parallel to Horse Guards Road.

To your right, beside Clive Steps, is the Churchill Museum and Cabinet War Rooms, telling the story of the legendary Sir Winston Churchill and the day-to-day decision making of the Second World War.

Carry on along this path, with a rustic lakeside cottage and Duck Island on your left. Soon you arrive at the Guards Division War Memorial, with the open space of Horse Guards Parade to your right. There are toilets a few yards ahead.

The Horse Guards originated in 1660, when Charles II, just restored to the throne, formed four regiments of cavalry for royal protection. To either side of Horse Guards Parade are the grand premises of Government: Cabinet Office, Foreign Office, Defence, Treasury, and Parliamentary offices. There is even a view of the rear of Downing Street's well-protected residences. On the left of the parade ground are the Old Admiralty Buildings, distinctively topped with green domes, while located near to the central archway is The Household Cavalry Museum. Guard-changing here is at 11:00 daily, 10:00 on Sundays.

At the War Memorial, turn left into St James's Park and keep going to the 'Inn the Park' café. Bear left here to follow the water's edge.

Favoured by royalty from the days when Henry VIII took the land from the Abbot of Westminster, serious attempts at landscaping St James's Park had to wait until the early 1600s. When Charles II returned as King he started transforming the marshy royal hunting ground into a park that he, and his subjects, could enjoy.

Right: St James's Park lake and fountain

James I had kept animals here, including crocodiles, camels, and an elephant, and also a selection of exotic birds along Birdcage Walk, and then Charles added avenues of trees and a long, straight canal. In 1664 the pelicans that are still a feature of the waterside today were given by the Russian Ambassador. Other unexpected birdlife here includes tawny owls, which breed here, and great spotted woodpeckers, whose staccato drumming you may hear in the treetops.

Above: Several pelicans are part of a multitude of water-loving birds that congregate in St James's Park

During the 1820s the park was redesigned in a more natural way, without the rigid straight lines, by John Nash. This famous architect in the days of the Prince Regent (later to become George IV) carried out many major schemes in London, including Regent Street, Regent's Park, and the Regent's Canal.

It is said that two oak trees that were blown down in the park during a storm in 1833 grew from acorns that King Charles had brought from the tree in which he hid at Boscobel.

At a bridge over the lake (there are toilets to the right here, and a chance to make a detour to St James's Palace) **keep ahead by the waterside.** If you wish to see St James's Palace, turn right to leave the park and cross The Mall, then go ahead along Marlborough Road towards Pall Mall, and turn left to the palace buildings.

Left: St James's Palace

Built in the 1530s, St James's Palace is a handsome red-brick building, or more accurately a collection of buildings. Apart from the sentry-guarded Tudor gatehouse, survivors of the original structure include the Chapel Royal, where regular church services are open to the public, and two Tudor rooms that escaped a disastrous fire in 1809. The complex includes Clarence House, London home of the Prince of Wales and his two sons, and apartments occupied by the Princess Royal and Princess Alexandra. The palace is much used for State occasions, being still the official residence of the Sovereign, and ambassadors have to present themselves here, to the Court of St James's.

Continuing on the main walk by the water's edge, when finally the path swings left before a high wall, turn right up a slope to The Mall.

Right: Crowds begin to gather by the sunlit Queen Victoria Memorial for a ceremonial occasion at Buckingham Palace

The Mall makes a good vantage point from which to view Buckingham Palace and the Queen Victoria Memorial. This eye-catching memorial has Queen Victoria facing east, with the pillar at her back topped by a gilt figure of winged Victory, with smaller gilded figures of Courage and Constancy beneath. Truth, Justice, and Motherhood are represented on the three other sides of the plinth.

Surrounding the central statue are more symbolic figures, with the majestic gates and balustrades by which you are standing all planned as a harmonious scheme. Although work started on the memorial in 1906, with the official opening by King George V in 1911, the whole job took until 1924 to complete. Knighted at the opening ceremony, the sculptor was Thomas Brock.

Above: Ceremonial guards process along The Mall

In the early 1600s the place where Buckingham Palace stands today contained a great number of mulberry trees, established by James I to encourage the silk industry. Later in the 17th century Arlington House occupied the site, and when this building was demolished in 1703, John Sheffield, Duke of Buckingham, had a red-brick mansion built here. George III was the first monarch to reside in Buckingham House, which did not achieve the title of Palace until rebuilt by John Nash in 1825–36. A stucco-covered east wing was added a few years later, by Edward Blore and Thomas Cubitt. Considered to be not in keeping with the grandeur of Queen Victoria's newly erected memorial, Sir Aston Webb (who was also responsible for the design of the memorial) created the Portland stone façade that you see today in 1913. As befits the official London residence of the Queen, the palace possesses 775 rooms, including 19 State rooms. The Archbishop of Canterbury has christened four royal babies in the Music Room: the Prince of Wales, the Princess Royal, the Duke of York, and Prince William.

Changing of the guard takes place at 11:30, every day in summer, and every other day in winter. Adjacent to the palace, The Queen's Gallery and the Royal Mews are both open to the public.

Cross The Mall at the pedestrian lights then follow the back of the stone balustrade as it curves round to the finely crafted Canada Gates. **At the gates turn right into Green Park on The Broad Walk, then after 90 yards, at the**

second junction, bear left. Stay on this broad path as it undulates its way through the length of the park, gradually converging on Piccadilly.

The Green Park, known as such because of its grassy aspect, is very pleasant, but unassuming. However, the park has a secret past, having been a royal deer-hunting ground in the 17th century, a place where duels were fought, and the venue for tremendous firework displays during national celebrations in the 18th and 19th centuries. It became a public park in 1826. The course of the long-forgotten Tyburn stream is thought to have been across the park. Flowing from the hills of Hampstead, through Marylebone and Mayfair, in Green Park it formed the Tyburn Pool, before continuing down the slope towards where Buckingham Palace now stands, and into the marshy area around Westminster.

As your path curves sharply to the left, **turn right to leave the park at Hyde Park Corner.** Turn left, then right to cross at the lights, heading for the Wellington Arch. **Go through the arch,** pausing to admire the massive iron gates and fluted Corinthian columns.

Right: Wellington Arch, marooned in the middle of Hyde Park Corner

The Wellington Arch is topped with a dramatic bronze statue sculpted by Adrian Jones, of Peace, winged and dominant, descending on the chariot of war. English Heritage are responsible for both Apsley House (open Tuesday-Sunday), and Wellington Arch (normally open Wednesday-Sunday), which contains exhibitions including London's smallest police station, and access to a balcony offering far-reaching views above and away from the traffic.

Everywhere your eye wanders on this stranded island amongst a roaring sea of traffic is yet another memorial to those who fought and died for our freedom today. Surrounding you are the Machine Gun Corps, Royal Artillery, New Zealand, and Australian war memorials, and taking pride of place, the Wellington Arch, with the 'Iron Duke' himself on horseback nearby. Arthur Wellesley, 1st Duke of Wellington, victor over Napoleon in 1815 at the Battle of Waterloo, and Prime Minister in 1828–30, lived in Apsley House (the building faced in golden-brown Bath stone to your right). The house, containing the Wellington Museum, is unique in that it is London's last great town house in which descendants of the famous owner still live, and yet is open to the public. At one time it stood at the end of a terrace of houses in Piccadilly, but all its near neighbours fell foul to road-widening.

Walk forward to the Royal Artillery Memorial and turn right to cross at the lights towards the archway giving access to Hyde Park. Stage One of your walk finishes here, with Hyde Park Corner station adjacent. There are toilets a few yards to the left.

Stage Two: Hyde Park Corner to Holland Park

Distance 4 miles. Intermediate distances: The Serpentine 1 mile, Kensington Gardens 2 miles, Kensington Church Street 3 miles.

Time 2½ hours.

Terrain Fairly level tarmac paths and pavements, short stretch of gravel path in Holland Park.

Refreshments The Dell, and The Lido cafés, both by The Serpentine; Kensington High Street and Church Street; Holland Park.

Toilets Hyde Park Corner, Hyde Park (by The Serpentine), Kensington Gardens, Hornton Street, near Kensington Library; Holland Park.

Transport Fare zones 1 & 2. Hyde Park Corner (Tube, bus), Knightsbridge (Tube, bus), High Street Kensington (Tube, bus), Kensington Olympia (train, Tube, bus), Holland Park (Tube, bus), Notting Hill Gate (Tube, bus).

Best time to do the walk As with Stage One, choose a bright, calm day.

Right: The Royal Artillery Memorial is one of Hyde Park Corner's sombre assembly of war memorials

The sheer volume of traffic hurtling around Hyde Park Corner is nothing new; even in the 1930s it was a busy gyratory system, handling 83,000 vehicles in a 12-hour period, which had risen to 120,000 by 1958. In the 21st century congestion charging, which sounds very much like going back to the days of toll-roads and turnpikes, became the fashionable solution.

Start at Hyde Park Corner (Piccadilly line, frequent buses). **Go through the gate in the archway** next to Apsley House to enter Hyde Park. Cross South Carriage Drive and then bear left to follow a shared path and cycle track for 50 yards, when you bear right to enter the Rose Garden.

Away to the right as you entered the park you may have noticed the giant bronze figure of Achilles by Sir Richard Westmacott, which was cast from twelve 24-pounder captured French guns. It serves as another monument to Wellington, and was unveiled in 1822. The elaborate entrance gates to the park at Queen Elizabeth Gate date from 1993.

In common with many of London's parks, Hyde Park first rose to prominence as a royal hunting-ground. Previously having belonged to the Abbey of Westminster, it passed into royal ownership at the Reformation in the 1530s, becoming another deer-park for Henry VIII to hunt in. One hundred years later it had become a public park; but in 1652 the Commonwealth Government sold it to a private owner, who charged admission. At about this time, Oliver Cromwell had a lucky escape when travelling through the park, when his horses became unruly, and he was thrown from his carriage. A pistol went off in his pocket, but with true British grit he was able to get up, and after having a little blood let, to carry on as normal.

Two gentlemen who did not have any luck, however, were Lord Mohun and the 4th Duke of Hamilton; they were both killed in a duel here in 1712.

You may still see horses in the park today on Rotten Row, the name probably derived from 'Route du Roi', for this was the original royal way from Hyde Park Corner to Kensington Palace.

Follow the path as it winds through the gardens, passing two attractive fountains, with a long arbour on your left. Keep on ahead after leaving the Rose Garden, past a neat parade of benches. **Bear right up a short slope,** then before reaching the roadway, turn left, with The Dell café on your right, to cross a wide bridge over The Dell.

Once over the bridge look out for a homely little inscription, placed in this most delightful spot, to Queen Caroline, wife of George II 'for whom the Long Water and Serpentine were created between 1727–31'. It is interesting to compare this humble monument to the fabulously decorative Albert Memorial which you can see, slightly off your route, a little further on.

Bear right to follow the bank of The Serpentine. Pass The Lido and café (there are toilets here), and then to your left, the much-discussed Diana, Princess of Wales Memorial Fountain, forever gushing around its smooth, granite circuit. Stick to the water's edge to **go under the Serpentine Bridge,** where

Right: George Rennie's Serpentine Bridge of 1826 divides the Serpentine from the Long Water

45

you leave Hyde Park and enter Kensington Gardens. Carry on ahead with a railed-off strip of woodland on your right.

At first reserved for royalty from the time when William III acquired Kensington Palace, Kensington Gardens had by the early 19th century become open to the general public. William and his wife Mary II, then Queen Anne, and later Queen Caroline, all added more land to the original 26 acre gardens, creating today's pleasant surroundings of lightly wooded informality, criss-crossed with smooth paths.

Above: Peter Pan, much-loved by children and tourists alike

There are several fine statues and monuments within the gardens, perhaps the best-known being Peter Pan, commissioned by J M Barrie from George Frampton in 1912, much climbed upon by young children, and in 1921 voted London's best statue; Physical Energy by G F Watts, 1904; and the Albert Memorial, described later on. There is also a youthful Queen Victoria, sculpted by her daughter, Princess Louise.

Soon you meet a path coming in from your left, which will be your route after a short diversion to the statue of Peter Pan. **Keep on ahead for 100 yards to see the statue, then retrace your steps to take this path (which will then be to your right), and then turn right again** to follow a straight tree-lined path to the statue of Physical Energy, a figure on horseback.

At this point, to your left down a broad avenue is the Albert Memorial, which is well worth seeing although it is not on your route. The gilded form of Prince Albert, Consort to Queen Victoria, sits comfortably amongst a superb assortment of carved figures, under a gilt and mosaic canopy, which is surmounted by an intricate, shining spire, rising to 180 ft. The Prince Consort was the driving force behind the Great Exhibition, held in Hyde Park in 1851, and the book he holds in his hand is an exhibition catalogue.

Above: a young Queen Victoria, sculpted by her daughter, Princess Louise

From the statue of Physical Energy, **maintain your direction by following the sign for Round Pond,** with Kensington Palace now firmly in your sights. When you arrive at the water's edge keep to the right-hand side to walk a half-circuit of the pond. At the other side, turn right to the statue of Queen Victoria. **Turn left here, on The Broad Walk** (there are toilets ¼ mile straight ahead), then **take the first right to arrive at the gates of Kensington Palace.** You have now crossed the western boundary of the City of Westminster to set foot in the Royal Borough of Kensington and Chelsea.

With his back to the palace, the richly attired figure of William III provides a good focal point for the symmetrical appeal of formal 17th-century splendour that you now see. William, unable because of his asthma to put up with the polluted air and damp surroundings of the royal palaces at St James's and Whitehall, paid 18,000 guineas in 1689 for what was then Nottingham House, then kept Sir Christopher Wren busy with the task of transforming the old house into a royal palace. William died in 1702, after which the palace was occupied by Queen Anne, and later Queen Caroline,

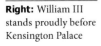

Right: William III stands proudly before Kensington Palace

both of whom made great improvements to Kensington Gardens and The Serpentine. From the time of George III royalty moved to Buckingham Palace and apart from the birth of Queen Victoria here in 1819, Kensington Palace declined in importance until more recent times when Princess Margaret, and Diana, Princess of Wales, lived here.

Turn around, and with the palace gates behind you, walk towards Kensington High Street and bear right to leave the gardens by a gate next to the Royal Garden Hotel. Turn right on Kensington High Street and pass the guarded entrance to Palace Green.

This wide street of well-protected ambassador's residences, which offers daytime public access, is actually part of the Crown Estates, and has the distinction of street lamps still lit by gas.

Press on ahead to the junction with Kensington Church Street. Cross at the lights and turn right to walk up Church Street, passing St Mary Abbots Church.

Victorian Gothic in style, the fine church of St Mary Abbots, designed by the famous architect Sir George Gilbert Scott and consecrated in 1872, is by far the most eye-catching sight in this area of wealth and quality. A trip to Kensington High Street used to mean a tour round the three department stores; Barker's, Derry and Toms, and Ponting's. Times have changed, and the High Street has kept up with the changes, but the church maintains its Victorian dignity, which is most apparent in the cool peace of its cathedral-like interior.

From Kensington Church Street take the first left into Holland Street. As you stroll along this charming street, look out for the numerous Courts, Walks, Mews, and Places leading off here and there; they are brimming over with character. Cross

Hornton Street (there are toilets to the left here, by the car park ramp, just past the library) and carry on past the functional bulk of the Town Hall. Cross to the right-hand pavement, and then at Campden Hill Road use the zebra crossing to continue ahead on Duchess of Bedford's Walk. **Cross Holland Walk to enter Holland Park.** Carry on straight ahead, passing the Youth Hostel and steps leading up to a glimpse of Holland House.

Peacocks, a Japanese water garden, formal gardens with a sub-tropical border, an arboretum, a wildlife pond, and a 'Wildernesse'; all these attractions plus an atmospheric, semi-ruined Jacobean mansion providing a backdrop to open-air summertime opera productions, are on offer at Holland Park. It is extraordinary that this popular and busy park remained a private estate, right here in the middle of London, until it was purchased by the London County Council from the 6th Earl of Ilchester in 1952. The Royal Borough of Kensington and Chelsea is now in charge, with the financial and practical help of the Friends of Holland Park.

Right: Formal gardens at Holland Park lead to 17th- century Holland House

Holland House was built for Sir Walter Cope around 1605–08, and was at first known as 'Cope's Castle'. His daughter Isabel married Sir Henry Rich, who in 1624 became the 1st Earl of Holland. Over the years, ownership of the house by various branches of the Rich, Edwardes, and Fox families culminated in the tenure of the 3rd Lord Holland, a time when visitors included such famous names as Disraeli, Byron, and Dickens.

The peak of entertaining was reached on 6 July 1939, when a dinner and ball were staged for King George VI and Queen Elizabeth. Following the outbreak of war, in September 1940 an incendiary bomb left the house burnt-out, after which it was decided to rebuild just parts of the old mansion. These attractive buildings can best be seen across the formal gardens, and as part of the Youth Hostel.

At the end of the café outdoor seating area, turn right to go through an arch, then bear left past a pond and fountain to go through a brick archway onto a terrace.

Turn right to leave the terrace through a brick opening, then bear half-right and then left between low wooden fences, after which you bear right to pass the Kyoto Garden (there are steps, and a ramp a few yards further on, up to this peaceful water-garden).

Keep ahead, now on a firm gravel track, and **at the first junction turn right.** Soon you will arrive at a meeting of paths, by a statue of Lord Holland. **Go across the little bridge** to the left of His Lordship, and then continue ahead, straight on at a crossing path, to descend a tarmac slope and **leave the park through an archway** onto the road called Holland Park. Turn right and walk to the T-junction with Holland Park Avenue.

With the noble statue of Saint Volodymyr, Ruler of

Ukraine 980–1015, for company on this corner, you have a choice; either walk a few yards to the left and cross at the traffic lights to the official end of the 'Parks and Palaces' walk at Holland Park station, or turn right on Holland Park Avenue, where a stroll of barely ten minutes will bring you to the cafés, pubs, and transport links of Notting Hill Gate.

Hopefully you have had a good time traversing some of London's most varied and beautiful parks; congratulations and well done.

Right: The impressive figure of St Volodymyr marks the end of your walk at Holland Park

3 Wilkes and Liberty!

Westminster to Clerkenwell in two stages

Linking a selection of the places that featured in the extraordinary life of outlandish 18th-century politician John Wilkes provides a very informal theme for this unique walk. From Westminster's grandeur, the route takes you past the dramatic riverside buildings of Vauxhall, to the Imperial War Museum, and then back over the Thames to visit the statue of John Wilkes in Fetter Lane. After this comes a short tour of historic Smithfield and then Clerkenwell, Wilkes' birthplace.

Stage One: Westminster to Waterloo

Distance 4 miles. Intermediate distances: Vauxhall Bridge 1 mile, Lambeth Walk 2 miles, St George's Circus 3 miles.

Time 2½ hours.

Terrain All paved and level except for some riverside steps, which are easily avoided.

Refreshments Near to the start of the walk, Horseferry Road has a choice of places. There are two or three cafés near Vauxhall station and in Kennington Lane, after which there are a few isolated cafés and pubs, until you reach Waterloo, Lower Marsh, and The Cut, which offer ample choice.

Toilets Westminster, Vauxhall bus station, Waterloo.

Transport Fare zones 1 & 2. Westminster (Tube, bus), Vauxhall (train, Tube, bus), Lambeth North (Tube, bus), Waterloo (train, Tube, bus), Waterloo East (train).

Best time to do the walk
At any time, but many cafés, shops and facilities may be closed on Sunday.

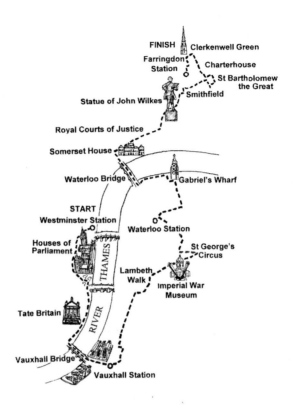

FINISH
Clerkenwell Green
Farringdon Station
Charterhouse
St Bartholomew the Great
Statue of John Wilkes
Smithfield
Royal Courts of Justice
Somerset House
Waterloo Bridge
Gabriel's Wharf
START
Westminster Station
Waterloo Station
Houses of Parliament
St George's Circus
THAMES
Lambeth Walk
Imperial War Museum
Tate Britain
RIVER
Vauxhall Bridge
Vauxhall Station

Right: Vauxhall City Farm provides a happy home for cattle, horses, sheep, goats, ducks and chickens

John Wilkes was born in 1727, into a world of wealth and privilege. His father was a member of the Distiller's Company, at a time when gin production was highly profitable. These were the days when it was said a man (or woman) could get 'drunk for a penny, or dead drunk for tuppence'.

Start at Westminster station (District, Circle, and Jubilee lines). Take Exit 3 for Houses of Parliament. You will emerge by the clock tower of Big Ben, where you turn left, away from the river, towards Parliament Square. Turn left here to walk past the Houses of Parliament and Westminster Hall. **Carry on past the public entrance to the Houses of Parliament, heading for the Victoria Tower and Millbank.**

Well educated but dissolute, Wilkes managed to be elected Member of Parliament for Aylesbury at the age of 30, and began to speak out against the bribery and corruption of the times. Soon his criticism extended to the Prime Minister, Lord Bute, who was supported by no less a person than King George III. The Establishment were enraged, Wilkes was arrested, and taken to the Tower. He appealed, won his case, successfully sued the Government for £1,000, and became a popular hero. When he held an open-air rally on Clerkenwell Green, a well-known radical meeting-place, an audience of several thousands gathered to hear his speech on Liberty, and the cry of 'Wilkes and Liberty!' was on everyone's lips.

In 1763, John Wilkes and a poet friend named Charles Churchill founded the satirical North Briton magazine, and in its pages Wilkes dared to criticise George III's opening speech to Parliament. Challenged to a duel by one of the King's supporters, Wilkes was injured, not long after which he was obliged to flee to France as an outlaw.

History surrounds you here; on your left, the Victorian

Gothic splendour of the Houses of Lords and Commons, with ancient Westminster Hall at their heart, collectively known as the Palace of Westminster; and to your right St Margaret's, Parliament's 'parish church' next to Westminster Abbey. Walk One, 'City to City' contains more details of these world-famous buildings.

Above: The Houses of Parliament, which John Wilkes entered at the tender age of 30 as MP for Aylesbury

When you arrive at the arched Sovereign's entrance at the Victoria Tower, pause for a moment to see, across the road, a patch of grass where a camera crew is normally in attendance to interview this or that politician, while in the background is the medieval Jewel Tower, where Edward III kept his jewels and finery.

Turn left into Victoria Tower Gardens, to be greeted by a statue of Emmeline Pankhurst. Walk towards Rodin's 'Burghers of Calais', heading for the riverside. Bear right to continue past the colourful Buxton memorial.

To your right, the monumental office blocks lining Millbank mostly originated in the early 1900s, while a little further on is the Millbank Tower, 32 storeys high, which was built 1960–63. Across the river there is an interesting contrast with the 1870s buildings of St Thomas's Hospital, and Lambeth Palace, parts of which are very old, including the red-brick 15th-century Gatehouse.

Continue ahead to climb the steps (or take the path to the right to avoid them) and cross the approach to Lambeth Bridge to descend more steps (again, easy to avoid) to walk through the last strip of Victoria Tower Gardens.

Lambeth Bridge was built to replace a horse-ferry that operated between here and Lambeth Palace, on the far shore. Unlike the ferryman's rowing boat, this was a large, flat, raft-like affair, capable of taking a 'coach and four'. The first bridge appeared in 1862; the one you see now dates from 1932.

Press on along Millbank, passing Millbank Tower and Tate Britain, opened in 1897 through the generosity of Sir Henry Tate. Previously the Millbank Penitentiary, said to be England's largest prison, stood here. When you reach a Henry Moore statue, 'Locking Piece', **bear left towards Vauxhall Bridge,** which is reached via steps (to avoid these, follow the pavement as it curves round to cross the bridge).

Before you cross the Thames, have a look at the giant figures that grace the bridge; four on each side. Facing downstream the figures represent Education, Local Government, Arts, and Science, while looking upstream are Engineering, Pottery, Agriculture, and Architecture. As you walk across, peep over the parapet at them; they are huge and imposing, but unseen by passers-by unless they happen to be in a boat. The first Vauxhall Bridge opened in 1816, and was replaced by

Left: 21st-century architectural statements; Vauxhall bus station, backed by strikingly imposing riverside flats

Right: The
figure of 'Arts' on
Vauxhall Bridge

today's bridge in 1906. It has the distinction of being
the first of London's bridges to carry trams.

Cross Vauxhall Bridge.

Framed by giant buildings, the view ahead is quite
striking; on the right, an architectural fantasy come
true, a mountain of glass-clad flats reaching up to a
group of weirdly shaped peaks; while on the left there is
the concrete and green glass fortress of MI6. Vauxhall
bus station, with its angular metal roof shooting out
into nowhere, completes this other-worldly scene.

For those with an interest in London's lost rivers, the
far bank will reveal a secret; the River Effra storm relief
channel, still trickling with a flow that emanates from
the hills of south London and makes its way here via
Brixton.

Once across the bridge, pass the MI6 building and maintain the same direction across Albert Embankment and through a tunnel under Vauxhall station, to continue along Kennington Lane.

From the central island of Albert Embankment, and a footbridge crossing just before the tunnel, there is access to Vauxhall train, Tube, and bus stations. There are toilets in the bus station.

Continue along Kennington Lane past the entrance to Spring Gardens. You will see one or two cafés here (try the Kennington Lane Café), and on the other side of the road St Anne's Catholic Church. Just past the church, **turn left to follow Tyers Street**.

Above: Less than a mile from Westminster's bustle, Vauxhall City Farm provides an oasis of tranquillity

Jonathan Tyers' name lives on in two local streets, Tyers Street and Jonathan Street. He was the dynamic manager of the Vauxhall Pleasure Gardens, described in Walk Four, 'Pleasure Grounds Old and New', the gardens having been on the site of Spring Gardens. Nowadays the pleasure is provided by Vauxhall City Farm, where cattle, horses, sheep, goats, and ducks appear to be quite happy in their inner-city home. Further up the street, the rural feeling is enhanced by a group of well-tended allotments.

Below: Preaching to the people – an open-air pulpit in Lambeth Walk

There are more allotments on the left, signalling the spot to **turn left to follow Laud Street.** At the end of this short street **turn right along Vauxhall Walk,** passing some interesting old dwellings and commercial premises. Continue past Pedlar's Park, a good picnic spot. Cross Black Prince Road and **carry on along Newport Street**, past the Beaconsfield contemporary art space, which started life in 1851 as the Lambeth Ragged School. Carry on past a line of railway arches, and then **at the T-junction with Old Paradise Street turn right, then after 75 yards first left to follow Lambeth Walk.**

Quieter now than in its pre-war heyday, Lambeth Walk, made famous in a music-hall song of pearly kings and queens, still displays echoes of the past; a terrace of old shop-fronts, nicely smartened up but lacking any clue as to their previous attractions, and a little further on, a gem of history; the Pelham Mission Hall, now the Henry Moore Sculpture Studio. There are two unusual features about this modest little building, tucked away in a sleepy back street; it sports an outdoor pulpit to really get the message to the people, and the foundation stone was laid by no less a personage than the Archbishop of Canterbury in 1910.

At the end of Lambeth Walk, turn right to follow Lambeth Road. Cross Kennington Road (one or two cafés and a pub to the left) and continue past the big guns of the Imperial War Museum.

Right: These giant guns give an indication of the impressive display to be seen at the Imperial War Museum

Tanks, rockets, land mines, and submarines; worldwide war zones, a stirring Holocaust exhibition, and the days and nights of the Blitz are amongst the frightening but fascinating displays in the Imperial War Museum. All this is contained in a former mental hospital; the Bethlehem Royal Hospital, or Bedlam as it was popularly known. It was built 1812–15 with the dome added 25 years later, and used to have large east and west wings; these were demolished in the 1930s to increase the size of Geraldine Mary Harmsworth Park. The patients were transferred at that time to Eden Park near Beckenham, and the museum, which had been squeezed into two galleries in South Kensington, came here in 1936.

Carry on ahead to cross St George's Road at the lights, with St George's Cathedral to your left. Soon you will arrive at St George's Circus.

Before this area became built up it was an open space known as St George's Fields, a place of many radical protests. It was here on 10 May 1768 that a gathering several thousand strong assembled in support of John Wilkes, who had been confined in the nearby King's Bench Prison after returning from exile. From the crowd there were chants of 'Wilkes and no King!' 'Damn the Government!' 'Wilkes and Liberty!' Fearing an attack on the prison, troops had been drafted in; they opened fire on the crowd, killing at least six people. This event went down in history as 'The Massacre of St George's Fields'.

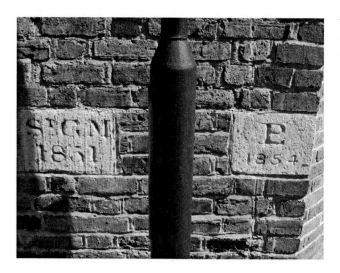

Left: Parish boundary markers, Emery Street

In 1771 the Portland stone obelisk was erected here. For many years, after being displaced, it stood in Geraldine Mary Harmsworth Park, and has only recently been returned to its true home, where the distances chiselled into its sides are once again accurate.

At St George's Circus, where Lambeth Road ends, turn sharp left to follow Westminster Bridge Road. Press on to the junction with St George's Road, then use the crossings to gain the right-hand pavement. To your left is Morley College, named after Samuel Morley MP, whose name is also on the 1873 foundation stone of the Lincoln Tower of Christ Church, just ahead.

A few yards past this junction turn right into Pearman Street, which has a massive red-brick and grey-clad modern block of flats on the corner. Follow this tree-lined thoroughfare of solid old dwellings (Emery Street, on the right, has two parish markers from the 1850s set into the wall).

At the T-junction with Waterloo Road, by the Living Space café, turn left to pass a deluxe children's playground, and then the Waterloo Millennium Green. To your right is the Old Vic Theatre. Cross Baylis Road and continue for 150 yards to the **end of Stage One at Waterloo station.**

Right: The Queen's Walk awaits you in Stage Two

Stage Two: Waterloo to Clerkenwell

Distance 4 miles. Intermediate distances: Waterloo Bridge 1 mile, Temple Bar 2 miles, Smithfield 3 miles.

Time 3 hours.

Terrain A 400 yard detour is necessary to avoid steps at Waterloo Bridge, and access from Ely Place (Holborn) to Ely Court is restricted by an upright bar, placed there many years ago to prevent horses from entering. This will only involve retracing your steps a very few yards. Smithfield and Clerkenwell have several cobbled streets, which can be avoided in some places.

Refreshments Plenty of choice around Waterloo, Lower Marsh, and The Cut, Gabriel's Wharf by the Thames, Fleet Street, Holborn, Clerkenwell, and Farringdon.

Toilets Waterloo station, Gabriel's Wharf, Oxo Tower, Strand (near the Royal Courts of Justice), Smithfield.

Transport Fare zone 1. Waterloo (train, Tube, bus), Waterloo East (train), Southwark (Tube, bus), Temple (Tube, bus), Barbican (train, Tube, bus), Farringdon (train, Tube, bus).

Best time to do the walk
Anytime that the mood takes you.

Left: A pretty terrace of cottages in Roupell Street, just a stone's throw from Waterloo station

Start at Waterloo station (Jubilee, Northern, Bakerloo, Waterloo & City lines, National Rail, frequent buses). **Take the exit for Waterloo Road, cross at the lights, then turn left and then right to follow Sandell Street.** At the end turn left under a bridge into Cornwall Road. Take the second right, Roupell Street, and press on to the end of this street of rustic old cottages. **At the junction with Hatfields turn left**, passing a lovingly tended, quite unexpected garden, and a sports pitch. Continue to the end of Hatfields, crossing Stamford Street on the way. **Turn left into Upper Ground,** then after 100 yards **turn right to walk through Bernie Spain Gardens to the riverside Queen's Walk, where you turn left.**

Take in the fine riverside panorama from here of the City, St Paul's, Somerset House, and two bridges: Waterloo and Blackfriars. To your right is the Oxo Tower, the novel way of publicising this meat-extract product cleverly designed to avoid planning restrictions on outdoor advertising. On the left is Gabriel's Wharf, an appealing huddle of craft shops, galleries, and cafés. There are toilets here and at Oxo Tower Wharf. As you progress along the Queen's Walk you will pass the stark outlines of the National Theatre, and one or two information panels describing the riverside scene. Second-hand books are laid out for sale under Waterloo Bridge, especially at weekends.

Do not go under Waterloo Bridge, instead climb the steps over to the left to walk across the bridge (to avoid the steps, a 200 yard diversion to the left is necessary; cross Upper Ground and take the rising ramp to then double back across the bridge). Once you are across the Thames, **pass Somerset House and turn right to follow the Strand.** There is an automatic toilet a short way along, and subterranean toilets a little further on.

Several wonderful buildings delight the eye here.

Somerset House takes its name from Edward Seymour, Duke of Somerset, who was executed in 1552, before his grandiose scheme was finished; it was later occupied by royalty, then by offices, and nowadays is a major tourist attraction. For a modest entrance fee you can enjoy the Gilbert Collection of decorative arts, the Courtauld Institute Gallery, and Russian art at the Hermitage Rooms, not to mention the fountain-filled courtyard and River Terrace.

The parish church of St Mary-le-Strand dates from 1725, built from designs by James Gibbs, and was one of the Queen Anne churches erected after the Fifty New Churches Act of 1711. It is the official church of the Women's Royal Naval Service (WRNS), and is reckoned to be one of London's finest 18th-century churches.

Above: St Mary-le-Strand stands on the original line of the beach, or 'strand', of the Thames

Fronted by statues of Gladstone, Sir Arthur Harris, and Lord Dowding, St Clement Danes is the central church of the Royal Air Force. Designed by Sir Christopher Wren, it was completed in 1682, with the steeple added by James Gibbs in 1719. Although this church lays claim to the 'Oranges and Lemons' of the nursery rhyme, there is another contender for this title; St Clement Eastcheap, in the City.

Behind the church is a statue of Doctor Samuel Johnson, lexicographer, biographer, wit, and the man who coined the phrase: 'When a man is tired of London he is tired of life; for there is in London all that life can afford'. In his house in Gough Square, just off Fleet Street, he produced in 1755 the first comprehensive English dictionary. Doctor Johnson's house is normally open to the public Monday-Saturday 11:00-17:30.

Continue along the Strand towards Temple Bar and Fleet Street. There are toilets in the central island by the Royal Courts of Justice.

Regularly featured on television news, the magnificent Royal Courts of Justice were designed by George

Edmund Street, and opened by Queen Victoria in 1882. Within its confines there are over 1,000 rooms, and three and a half miles of corridors, one of which is known as the 'Chicken Run'. Official tours of this Victorian Gothic building take place on the first and third Tuesdays of each month.

Keep on ahead as the Strand leads into Fleet Street.

At Temple Bar the obelisk that graces the road marks the spot where one of the eight gates of the City used to stand. Narrow openings in these ancient structures impeded traffic, and they were all demolished except for this one; it was bought by Sir Henry Meux and carefully rebuilt as a gateway to his mansion at Theobald's Park in Hertfordshire. In 2004 Temple Bar returned to the City, and is now at the entrance to Paternoster Square, next to St Paul's Cathedral.

Right: A fearsome dragon leaves you in no doubt that you are entering the City of London at Temple Bar

Unique remnants of another gateway, this time Ludgate, are on show on the other side of Fleet Street at St Dunstan in the West Church. This building of 1833, which replaced a medieval church on this site, has two muscular figures, high up in a canopy, that move to strike the bells with heavy clubs every quarter of an hour. There are statues of King Lud and his two sons, hidden away in a porch beneath a figure of Queen Elizabeth dating from 1586, all from the old gate which was demolished in 1760. A square tower topped with an octagonal lantern, and a fine 17th-century clock, completes this interesting repertoire.

Back on your side of the road Inner Temple Lane, with its gatehouse built in 1684, has for a next door neighbour a survivor of the Great Fire of London; Prince Henry's Room, built in 1610, which also houses the Samuel Pepys Exhibition. Entrance is free, and opening hours are Monday-Saturday 11:00-14:00.

After passing Prince Henry's Room and Ye Olde Cock Tavern, cross at the traffic lights to turn left along Fetter Lane. At the junction with New Fetter Lane, cross to the central island.

Now you can get an idea of the bold effrontery of John Wilkes, just by the look on his face, as he stands here on a plinth inscribed:

'A Champion of English Freedom
John Wilkes
1727–1797
Member of Parliament
Lord Mayor'

This is London's only cross-eyed statue, an honest appraisal of a man who once said that when meeting an attractive lady he could 'talk past his face in twenty minutes'. It was sculpted by James Butler RA and unveiled in 1988.

Wilkes did eventually help to bring about major constitutional changes, making Parliament less

Right: John
Wilkes holding
forth to passers-by
in Fetter Lane

secretive and more accountable, and reducing press censorship. As the years passed and he mellowed with age, he became less of a thorn in the side of the Government, eventually achieving high office as Lord Mayor of London in 1774. His embracing of the Establishment seems to have been complete by 1780, the year of the Gordon Riots, when he personally took charge of the security of the Bank of England, shooting some rioters when they attacked London Bridge, and throwing others into the Thames.

Bear left along Fetter Lane, turn right at Holborn **then left** at Holborn Circus to **follow Hatton Garden** for 50 yards, crossing to the right-hand side, to then go **through a doorway on the right into Ely Court,** leading to the Mitre Tavern.

As you join Holborn, to your left is the impressive red-brick Prudential Assurance building, the origins of which date from a smaller structure of 1879 designed by Alfred Waterhouse. Furnival's Inn used to occupy the site, and Charles Dickens started 'Pickwick Papers' while living there. At Holborn Circus is a statue of Prince Albert, on horseback, raising his hat; this is sometimes called 'London's politest statue'. Hatton Garden, known for many years as the centre of London's jewellery trade, recalls Sir Christopher Hatton, a favourite of Queen Elizabeth I, who in 1576 appropriated a large part of the palace of the Bishops of Ely, which stood here. The Mitre Tavern was built for the palace's servants, and in the bar there is a piece of a cherry tree around which Queen Elizabeth is said to have danced. As you emerge from Ely Court into Ely Place you are entering a little piece of Cambridgeshire, aloof from its city surroundings, and guarded by a beadle in his neat gatehouse. Here you will find St Etheldreda's Chapel, a 13th-century place of Catholic worship, with a crypt which, although now a place of peace and prayer, has in bygone times been a prison, store-house, and even a wine vault.

Ely Court leads through to Ely Place, passing the upright horse-barrier mentioned at the start (to avoid this, return to Holborn and turn left). **Turn right to Charterhouse Street** (or a few yards left to see St Etheldreda's Chapel), then turn left, downhill. There is an automatic toilet opposite. Continue down into the dip where the River Fleet once flowed, passing Saffron Hill on the left. **Cross Farringdon Road** and continue past the various buildings of Smithfield Market. At the traffic lights, cross to the right to **walk through the centre of the market** on Grand Avenue.

Above: Horse barrier at Ely Court, leading to the Mitre tavern

Painted in authentic Victorian hues of magenta, viridian, and violet, the London Central Meat Market opened in 1868. It was designed by Sir Horace Jones, the City Architect, a man who could also claim credit for Leadenhall Market, Tower Bridge, and other major city schemes. Apart from the cast-iron arches, which not only look good but help with ventilation, the construction is of Kentish red brick with Portland stone decoration. Underground there is a cavernous

Right: Early morning sun brightens the scene at Smithfield Meat Market

space in which meat-laden trains used to connect with the main line. On the four corners are domed towers; these used to be pubs, which along with other local hostelries such as The Hope and the Fox and Anchor would serve thirsty porters and market workers from the early hours of the morning.

Before 1855 when the market in live animals moved a few miles north to Copenhagen Fields, Smithfield (the 'Smooth-Field') had been for centuries an open area where all manner of sports and pastimes went on. Smithfield Fair, a free-and-easy event outside the strict jurisdiction of the City Corporation, was nevertheless opened each year by the Lord Mayor. When John Wilkes held this post in 1774 he not only opened the proceedings, but stepped down from his gilded coach and visited every booth on the field.

Cross Long Lane to West Smithfield and go

ahead for 70 yards to the Gatehouse of St Bartholomew the Great. There are toilets on the other side of the road.

St Bartholomew's Church and Hospital have their origins in the 12th century, having been founded by Rahere, courtier and jester to Henry I, who vowed to build a church after surviving a bout of malaria while on a pilgrimage to Rome. The hospital has some wonderful paintings by William Hogarth, and a museum containing an absorbing display of medical memorabilia. On the outside wall is an inscription that mentions the founding by Rahere in 1102, the refounding by Henry VIII in 1546, plus memorials to some of those who met a grisly end on the 'Smooth Field'. Further along is a rare statue of King Henry VIII, and just inside the hospital gateway is the ancient and interesting church of St Bartholomew the Less. St Bartholomew the Great, entered through a 13th-century archway, with a Tudor gatehouse above on which a depiction of St Bartholomew features, is one of London's oldest and most atmospheric places of worship. However the building has the most extraordinary history, parts of it having been divided up into houses, and at other times used as a smithy, a lace and fringe workshop, and a printing works.

Retrace your steps 20 yards to turn right into Cloth Fair. Continue along this quiet lane, passing a gate giving access to the garden occupying the area that was once the nave of St Bartholomew's Church. Once past the church, **turn left opposite Kinghorn Street** down a footway. Cross East Passage to emerge in Long Lane. Cross a few yards to the left to go **straight ahead on Hayne Street**, passing a charming old house, 'The Cottage', half-way along. At Charterhouse Square cross straight over, or use the zebra crossing a few yards to the left, to go through a set of gates into the cobbled square. Keep ahead, then right, to the old gateway of 'Sutton's

Hospital in Charterhouse'. Tours take place between April and August, pre-booked, for a fee.

Charterhouse dates back to the 1370s when Sir Walter de Manny founded an Order of Carthusian monks here, in memory of the lives lost in the Black Death of 1348–49. In 1611 the buildings were sold to Thomas Sutton, who established a school and almshouses. The school eventually moved to Godalming, in Surrey, where it occupies an extensive and beautiful location to this day, while the almshouses are still here.

Facing the old arched gateway, turn left to leave the square through another gateway onto Charterhouse Street. On the right is the Arts and Crafts style, tile-fronted Fox and Anchor pub of 1898. Now with the Meat Market buildings on your left, at the traffic lights turn right to St John Street. Cross to the left-hand side (not the extreme left, Cowcross Street) and carry on, bearing left into St John's Lane.

Hick's Hall used to stand in the centre of St John Street, explaining the extra-wide road where bikes now park. It was built as a courthouse, paid for by magistrate Sir Baptist Hicks in 1612, and had a room where bodies of criminals were dissected by medical students. In 1660 the Hall witnessed the trial of the 29 regicides who had signed the death warrant of King Charles I.

Follow St John's Lane to St John's Gate.

You may have noticed Passing Alley on the right; this is perhaps a politer spelling than its old name. A few yards after this is the gateway to the once-wealthy, 10-acre Priory of the Order of St John of Jerusalem, Clerkenwell. Founded in 1140 as the English headquarters of the Knights Hospitallers, crusaders who were active in Jerusalem, the Order was dissolved by Henry VIII in 1540. Over the years there were many and varied occupants of the buildings, including Queen Elizabeth I's Master of the Revels, and in the 18th century, the Gentleman's Magazine. Probably today's most familiar

Right: The Three Kings is one of Clerkenwell's unusual and interesting pubs

Left: St John's Gate was built by Prior Thomas Docwra in 1504

association would be St John Ambulance, which was established here. St John's Gate was built in 1504 by Prior Thomas Docwra, and offers guided tours, and a museum, open 10:00–17:00 Monday-Friday, 10:00–16:00 Saturday (closed Bank Holiday weekends).

Go through St John's Gate into St John's Square. Cross Clerkenwell Road to continue to the other side of the square.

Straight ahead of you, in the right-hand corner, a modern office building sits on the site of Israel Wilkes's mansion, birthplace of John Wilkes. All that remains of the Priory Church of St John, which includes a rare 12th-century crypt, is on your right. It was here in 1747 that John Wilkes married Mary Meade, a rich but plain heiress. Unfortunately not a successful match, it did however produce a daughter, Polly, the apple of her father's eye. In the National Portrait Gallery there is a painting of father and daughter gazing affectionately at one another.

Continue to the far side of the square and walk through Jerusalem Passage to Aylesbury Street. Note the corner wall-plaque to Thomas Britton, the 'Musical Coalman', who

entertained famous musicians, including Handel, at his musical gatherings here.

Cross over and turn left, crossing Sekforde Street (where you can turn right for Young's real ale at the Sekforde Arms) to Clerkenwell Green, then take a **right turn into Clerkenwell Close** to St James's Church and the Three Kings pub. The cheeky pub sign displays a Clerkenwell version of this name: Elvis, King Kong, and Henry VIII.

Local architect James Carr designed St James's Church, which was completed in 1792. If you have time, do go inside; the interior is a treasure-trove of very old memorials and elaborate gilt-lettered lists of past benefactors to the parish.

Retrace your steps to grassless Clerkenwell Green, where your route bears right, across the green, to the solitary splendour of the Old Sessions House, now the London Masonic Centre.

Built in 1779–82, with relief sculptures by Joseph Nollekens, the former Middlesex Sessions House was rumoured to have tunnels through which those unlucky enough to be sentenced to transportation were taken straight out to a waiting ship on the river. The ghost of a weeping woman, whose lover faced this fate, is said to haunt the building.

Above: St James's Church is tucked away in a green and peaceful corner of Clerkenwell

If you would like to see the Clerk's Well which gave this district its name, before you cross the green bear right to Farringdon Lane, and peer down through the window of Well Court to get a glimpse. For a closer look, try joining one of the regular guided walks of the area, where the guide will often have keys to places of interest. In medieval times members of the Parish Clerks enacted religious 'mystery' plays every year at this and other wells hereabouts. The local spring water was particularly healthy and also good for brewing and distilling; Booth's gin factory in Turnmill Street only ceased production a few years ago.

Clerkenwell Green has been a place of radical protest for centuries, especially in the 18th and 19th centuries when the surrounding streets were crammed with artisans and working people, many of them on the breadline. It was a natural choice for John Wilkes to give a speech here on 'Liberty' before his flight to Paris as an outlaw in 1764. Also of interest and well worth a visit, the Marx Memorial Library, containing a room where Lenin worked, is at number 37a.

From the Old Sessions House cross Clerkenwell Road half-left to Britton Street, using the crossing just a few yards to the right to get to the other side of this busy road. Continue along Britton Street.

The early 1700s are still evident in a few original houses here, some with high weaver's windows in the roof, to provide better light to work by. On the left, 1720 is the date proclaimed by the quaint Jerusalem Tavern, a favourite Clerkenwell watering-hole. High above you on the right is a frieze decorating an arcaded front that was formerly part of Booth's Distillery. A little further along, at number 44 on the corner of Albion Place, is a somewhat zany house designed by Piers Gough, and formerly the home of journalist and indefatigable long-distance walker Janet Street-Porter.

Opposite Albion Place, with gardens and a seating area on the corner, turn right to follow Benjamin Street. At the end of this narrow back-way, turn left into Turnmill Street. Farringdon station, and the end of your walk, is on the right, in Cowcross Street.

Steeped in history, this part of London fascinates at every turn; long ago mills used the power of the Fleet River here in Turnmill Street, many years before Farringdon station appeared on London's first underground railway, which opened in 1863. Cowcross Street recalls the chaotic procession of animals that passed this way, bound for Smithfield Market, until the live animal market moved in 1855. On the corner of Cowcross Street is the Castle pub, unique in having been granted a pawnbroker's licence by King George IV, after being helped out when he required some ready funds following an unprofitable night's gambling. Three golden balls are still displayed outside the pub.

In John Wilkes's day the scene would have been quite different; industry, animals, smoke, smells, and noise. Nowadays this place of offices, pubs, and restaurants is more welcoming, and makes an interesting conclusion to the 'Wilkes and Liberty!' walk. Well done, now you can raise a celebratory glass of your favourite tipple, or perhaps spend a while exploring the esoteric delights of Clerkenwell and Smithfield.

Right: Looking from the 'nave' of St Bartholemew the Great

Pleasure Grounds Old and New

Vauxhall to Camden Lock in three stages

A journey from the Lambeth riverside site of the old-time Vauxhall Pleasure Gardens, passing the seat of power at Westminster and Whitehall, and continuing through Theatreland and then Bloomsbury, home of the British Museum. There is a complete change of scene as the walk weaves through King's Cross and past the London Canal Museum, discovering little-known backwaters in this tangle of traffic and travellers, before visiting the well-kept streets of Barnsbury on the way to the extraordinary bazaar that is Camden Lock, centred around old wharves on the Regent's Canal.

Stage One: Vauxhall to Trafalgar Square

Distance 2 miles. Intermediate distance: Victoria Tower Gardens 1 mile.

Time 1½ hours.

Terrain Paved and level, with a few easily avoided steps.

Refreshments Some cafés near Vauxhall station, tea room at the Museum of Garden History, and on the nearby riverbank. Plenty of choice around Trafalgar Square and Charing Cross.

Toilets Vauxhall bus station, Parliament Street, Trafalgar Square.

Transport Fare zones 1 & 2. Vauxhall (train, Tube, bus), Westminster (Tube, bus), Charing Cross (train, Tube, bus).

Best time to do the walk Pick a warm, clear day when you can admire the river views and fine buildings.

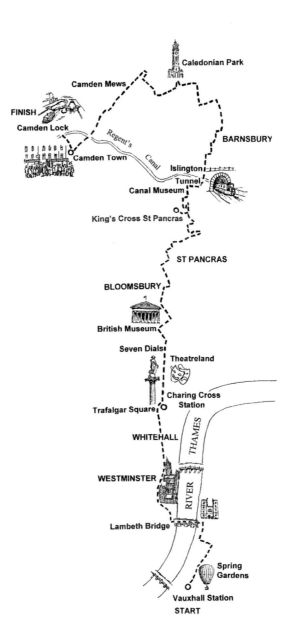

Caledonian Park

Camden Mews

FINISH

Camden Lock

Regent's Canal

Camden Town

BARNSBURY

Islington
Tunnel

Canal Museum

King's Cross St Pancras

ST PANCRAS

BLOOMSBURY

British Museum

Seven Dials

Theatreland

Charing Cross
Station

Trafalgar Square

THAMES

WHITEHALL

WESTMINSTER

RIVER

Lambeth Bridge

Spring
Gardens

Vauxhall Station
START

E merging from the station at Vauxhall can be a shock to the system. From being cosily ensconced on train or Tube, dozing or reading, you are suddenly surrounded by madly whirling traffic, your every move watched by the huge green-windowed MI6 building on the Embankment. You need to escape, and fast!

Start at Vauxhall station (trains from Waterloo or Clapham Junction, Victoria line, and buses from all parts). Take the South Lambeth Road exit from the station and turn left (from the Tube station, **take exit 3 and then turn right through a tunnel, following signs for Spring Gardens.** This will bring you to the South Lambeth Road rail exit). Cross Kennington Lane at the lights to the Royal Vauxhall Tavern opposite. Turn right, then immediately left through a metal arch into Spring Gardens.

The name Vauxhall may have derived from 'Falkes Hall', a manor house built here by Falkes de Breaute in the 13th century. This gentleman obviously chose a good spot, as 400 years later, surrounded by open fields and markets, the 'New Spring Gardens' opened to the public, offering visitors walks amongst the simple delights of flowers, birdsong and fresh air, and a chance to escape the city. Samuel Pepys often came to 'Foxhall' by boat to hear the nightingale sing, and to enjoy an occasional clandestine female encounter.

With the opening of Westminster Bridge in 1750, and patronage of royalty and aristocracy who delighted in the musical temple, orchestra, and lamp-lit walks that were added by the energetic manager, Jonathan Tyers, success was assured, and in later years balloon ascents and firework displays increased the excitement, which reached a crescendo in 1827 with a re-enactment of the Battle of Waterloo, involving 1,000 horse and foot soldiers.

Gradually the surrounding fields began to be replaced

by factories and houses as London spread, and the gardens finally closed in 1859, after entertaining the public for nearly 200 years.

Right: Spring Gardens, site of the Vauxhall Pleasure Gardens

Follow the tarmac path ahead and after 60 yards fork left. Continue straight on to the end of the gardens, where you keep going in the same direction along Vauxhall Walk. Carry on past the Vauxhall Gardens Community Centre and on the right, the old frontage of Horatio Myers Bedstead Works to eventually reach the junction with Black Prince Road at the Queen's Head café/pub, with Arden House on the right. Turn left here to **pass under the railway bridge.**

Set in the brickwork of the bridge are a series of Doulton plaques commemorating the Black Prince, son of Edward III. Famous for his fearless soldierly deeds in the 14th century, he owned land in this area.

After 150 yards, turn right into Lambeth High Street.

The ornate Victorian Gothic building on the corner of Lambeth High Street is the last vestige of Doulton's huge Lambeth pottery, and closer inspection will reveal an extraordinary façade of terracotta and tile ornamentations. Apart from pots and drainpipes, Victorian industry in this area included vinegar distillers, bone boilers, glass manufacturers, and boat-builders. The Vauxhall Iron Works produced its first car here in 1903. Imagine the polluting effect all these belching chimneys had, especially on the gardens.

Left: Surviving evidence of Doulton's extensive Lambeth pottery

Follow Lambeth High Street, passing the Windmill pub. At Lambeth Road, cross over and then turn left to the Museum of Garden History opposite, housed in the former St Mary's Church.

Well worth seeing, this interesting old church has memorials to Captain Bligh, who famously survived a mutiny on board his ship the 'Bounty', and also to John Tradescant and his son, international plant collectors and gardeners to Charles I. The museum has an abundance of gardening memorabilia, a fine display of prints depicting horticulture through the ages, and a café. Open 10:30–17:00 Tuesday–Sunday.

The secretive, ancient building next door courts little attention, other than a casual admiration of the mellow red brick gatehouse. Passers-by may have no idea that this is Lambeth Palace, London home of the Archbishops of Canterbury for eight hundred years. Until the Industrial Revolution, this area possessed only this palace, St Mary's Church, huts for the local fisherfolk and a few dwellings. The advantages for such an important religious foundation were seclusion and privacy, but with easy river access to Westminster and the City.

Right: Glowing in the evening sun, this is the 15th-century gatehouse to Lambeth Palace

However, London could be a violent city, and in the Peasant's Revolt of 1381 Wat Tyler's rebels plundered the palace, burning all the books in the process. Later, during the Commonwealth period, the palace was

attacked and badly damaged. It was threatened again during the Gordon Riots of 1780. No wonder it has retreated into anonymous isolation behind those secure walls.

Go past the church and palace, and **cross Lambeth Palace Road at the lights.** Now **cross Lambeth Bridge to turn sharp right** into Victoria Tower Gardens.

Left: Lambeth Bridge affords a fine view of the Houses of Parliament

Follow the riverside, pausing to admire the richly decorated Buxton Memorial to the 1833 Abolition of Slavery Act, until near the end of the gardens you bear left, past Rodin's 'The Burghers of Calais', to **emerge by Victoria Tower. Turn right, towards Parliament Square.**

Passing the Houses of Parliament, it is difficult not to be impressed by the rich ornamentation on this imposing Victorian edifice. What you see now is the result of a competition held to design a new building in the Gothic style, after a disastrous fire in 1834. Out of 97 entries, Charles Barry was the winner, and together with A W Pugin, who was responsible for the wealth of Gothic detail, created this palace with its 1,100 rooms, 100 staircases and two miles of passages. Barry

Above: Victoria Tower

received a knighthood for his hard work from Queen Victoria after she performed the opening ceremony in 1852. Severe wartime damage led to the House of Commons being rebuilt by the eminent architect Sir Giles Gilbert Scott; it was completed in 1950, mostly to the original plans.

Across the road are Westminster Abbey and St Margaret's Church, both watched over with some disdain by Oliver Cromwell from his plinth in front of Westminster Hall. This magnificent building has been in continuous use for over nine hundred years, since the time of William Rufus, and has survived fire, flood and the ravages of death watch beetle.

Weave your way through the camera-wielding tourists and **cross Bridge Street to continue in the same direction along Parliament Street** (there are toilets in the subway here). Continue along Whitehall to Trafalgar Square.

Above: From a window of the Banqueting House Charles I stepped onto the scaffold to meet his fate

Massive and powerful-looking Government offices line Whitehall, with Downing Street and Horse Guards of particular interest. The oldest and most eye-catching building is the Banqueting House, on the corner of Horse Guards Avenue. Designed by Inigo Jones, Surveyor to the King's Works, it was completed in 1622 as part of the great Whitehall Palace, the rest of which burnt down in 1698. It was from a first-floor window here that Charles I emerged on a cold January morning in 1649 to meet his fate on the scaffold, wearing two shirts so that he did not shiver and appear to be afraid. A plaque above the door recalls the event. The Banqueting House is normally open 10:00-17:00 Monday-Saturday.

At the top of Whitehall look out for a bronze statue, cast in 1633, of King Charles on horseback, on his own little island site. After his execution Cromwell ordered its destruction, and a brazier by the name of Rivett was entrusted with the job. He then proceeded to make a fortune from the sale of knick-knacks and trinkets supposedly made from the broken-up statue, which in fact he had somehow managed to conceal. At the Restoration of Charles II in 1660 Rivett proved, understandably, extremely reluctant to give it back.

Dominated by Nelson's Column, before you now is Trafalgar Square, where the first stage of your walk ends at the junction with the Strand (there are toilets in the north-west corner of the square). For Charing Cross station, cross Northumberland Avenue, then bear right into the Strand, with the station on your right.

Left: Lord Nelson is master of the scene in Trafalgar Square

Stage Two: Trafalgar Square to King's Cross

Distance 3 miles. Intermediate distances: Russell Square 1 mile, Argyle Street 2 miles.

Time 2 hours.

Terrain Paved and level, one cobbled street.

Refreshments Plenty of choice in Charing Cross, St Martin's Lane, Monmouth Street, and Great Russell Street. Café and perfect picnic venue at Russell Square. Marchmont Street in Bloomsbury has some cafés, and at walk's end the variety of venues around King's Cross should satisfy most tastes.

Toilets Trafalgar Square, Russell Square, Argyle Street (Euston Road).

Transport Fare zone 1. Charing Cross (train, Tube, bus), Leicester Square (Tube, bus), Russell Square (Tube, bus), King's Cross/ St Pancras (train, Tube, bus).

Best time to do the walk Anytime, but some facilities may be closed on Sundays.

Left: The Coliseum is next door to the Chandos pub, which sports a barrel-rolling porter at work

Start in Trafalgar Square, at the junction with the Strand, continuing from Stage One. Maintain the same northerly direction, with St Martin-in-the-Fields Church on your right. Keep to the right of Edith Cavell's statue, cross St Martin's Place, and **go forward along St Martin's Lane.**

Now, you stride into a new and distinct world: Theatreland. On your right the Coliseum, home of the English National Opera, exhibits an extravagant display of Edwardian decoration. For the next half-mile the various shows do their best to entice you through the door.

At the traffic lights at Long Acre, continue into Upper St Martin's Lane, which in turn becomes Monmouth Street. Continue straight ahead, passing the roundabout at Seven Dials, to join Shaftesbury Avenue.

Peek briefly up the unpromising West Street and you will discover the renowned Ivy restaurant, opposite which is St Martin's Theatre, still showing 'The Mousetrap' after more than fifty years. Back in Monmouth Street, the Two Brewers pub makes much of its 'English' menu, a pleasant surprise in these cosmopolitan surroundings.

Next is Seven Dials, where you can perch beneath the sundial and watch the world go by. If you can only count six dials, add the shadow from the column itself, and you have the seventh. Don't stop for too long, though; there are more miles to do yet. As you join Shaftesbury Avenue, Arthur Beale's interesting nautical shop seems oddly placed, so far from the sea.

Above: Seven Dials, a magnet for shoppers and tourists

Continue ahead to cross High Holborn. Pass the drinking fountain on your right, and then cross left at the lights to bear left up Shaftesbury Avenue, past the Bloomsbury Central Baptist Church. Keep ahead over New Oxford Street into Bloomsbury Street. **Take the first left into Streatham Street** for a brief digression to see Parnell House.

Clean and respectable as this area is now, you have just passed through what was, in Charles Dickens's time, the notorious St Giles' Rookery, a poverty-stricken slum. In several parts of inner London these rookeries were only cleared with the building of new roads, in this case New Oxford Street.

Thirty yards down Streatham Street is Parnell House, an 1850 block of 'Model Houses For Families' designed by the enlightened architect Henry Roberts. It was way ahead of its time, being light, airy and fireproof, warm and dry, and an escape from squalor for the lucky families selected to live here.

Retrace your steps to Bloomsbury Street, turn left, then cross right at the lights to Great Russell Street, which you take, passing the British Museum.

Right: Visitors flock to see the British Museum

At this point you can't miss the grandiose presence of the British Museum, which originated in 1753 with the purchase of physician Sir Hans Sloane's collection of 80,000 objects. This expense, plus the cost of a suitable building in which to house the collection (Montague House), required a public lottery to help raise the necessary funds.

As time passed, collections from far and wide of antiquities, books and manuscripts, coins, natural objects, and particularly the extensive library amassed by George III and the famous Elgin Marbles, created a pressing need for new buildings which have been added over the years. Montague House was swept away, and replaced by the present structure of 1842–7, with an impressive pediment-topped façade of Ionic columns that faces you across the courtyard.

In the 1950s there were plans to remove the buildings opposite the museum so that the viewer could take in the grandeur from a distance, but thankfully for the building's residents this did not happen.

The British Museum is open from 10:00–17:30, with some of the galleries opening late on Thursday and Friday.

At the end of the museum complex, turn left into Montague Street. Halfway along, cross over to the right-hand side and peep through some ornate metal gates to get a glimpse of one of London's hidden garden squares, some of which can be seen during the annual 'Open Garden Squares' weekend. **At Russell Square, cross diagonally,** passing the central fountain,to the north-east corner of the square (there is an automatic toilet here). Cross to the red brick and terracotta Hotel Russell, **turn left and then immediately right into Bernard Street, then take the second left into Marchmont Street.**

On your right is the 1960s Brunswick Centre, a 'mega structure' of flats, shops, restaurants, and a cinema. Marchmont Street has some interesting shops and, with its neighbouring streets, forms a friendly 'village'.

Carry on ahead, crossing Tavistock Place. Take the next **right into Leigh Street**, and at the end, **left into Judd Street then right into Cromer Street.**

Above: Marchmont Street is lined with independent shops of every description

Above: The
Brunswick Centre

Here are the aromas of a great many people living cheek-by-jowl; cooking, soap-suds, a waft of beer from the corner pub. On the left are Tonbridge Houses, erected by the East End Dwellings Co Ltd in 1904. Now you have left Bloomsbury for St Pancras, which is soon evident in the proliferation of small hotels, presumably here to serve the needs of a multitude of rail travellers.

Take the second left into Whidborne Street, which arrives at a T-junction with Argyle Street. Now bear right to **continue into Argyle Square** (or left for toilets which are in the St Pancras Library, at the top of Argyle Street).

You may notice on the corner the unlikely sight of a small communal garden, complete with a beehive and a small pond. In Argyle Square there are examples of a local speciality: faded Georgian houses with bags of character, which are steadily being renovated after decades of neglect, as the area comes up in the world. Here and in the nearby Regent Square you will find trees, shade and benches to give your feet a break.

At the end of Argyle Street, cross first Gray's Inn Road and then Swinton Street at the traffic lights, to continue ahead on Swinton Street's left-hand pavement. **At King's Cross Road, go left then left again into Wicklow Street.**

This cobbled, insignificant little backwater has for interest main line and underground trains rumbling through a cutting below your feet, and Wicklow Mill on the left. Could this mill be a reminder of bygone days when there were many springs and streams in this area, feeding the long-forgotten Fleet River?

Continue to the end of Wicklow Street, crossing Britannia Street on the way. **At the T-junction, turn right into St Chad's Place,** which soon becomes a covered passageway. Follow this to the left and **emerge on King's Cross Road. Turn left,**

**then immediately cross King's Cross Road
and then Pentonville Road at the lights, to
Northdown Street, which is opposite.** This is
the end of Stage Two, where a left turn will take you to
King's Cross rail and Tube stations.

Left: Keystone
Crescent is tucked
away near King's
Cross station

Stage Three: King's Cross to Camden Lock

Distance 3½ miles. Intermediate distances: Barnsbury 1 mile, Caledonian Park 2 miles.

Time 2-2½ hours.

Terrain Pavement or tarmac paths, except for the cobbled and uneven surface of Camden Mews, which is easily avoided.

Refreshments King's Cross, Caledonian Road, a pub and café in Barnsbury, plenty of choice in Camden Town.

Toilets King's Cross station, Camden Town. No public toilets in between. The café or pub at Barnsbury, both of which are ideal re-fuelling stops, may provide the answer.

Transport Fare zones 1 & 2. King's Cross/ St Pancras (train, Tube, bus), Caledonian Road and Barnsbury (train, bus), Caledonian Road (Tube, bus), Camden Road (train, bus), Camden Town (Tube, bus).

Best time to do the walk
If you want to see Camden Lock Market in full swing, go at the weekend; otherwise, the walk is enjoyable at any time.

Right: Parish boundary markers in Keystone Crescent

Start at the junction of Northdown Street and Pentonville Road, continuing from Stage Two (if you are starting from King's Cross station, turn left out of the station, cross York Way and then Caledonian Road, to the start). **Follow Northdown Street until it meets Caledonian Road, turn left then left again into Keystone Crescent,** a little old street lined with compact but charming houses, with numbers 14/15 and 18 sporting parish boundary markers. At the end **turn right and cross at the lights to go half-right up Balfe Street.** Keystone Crescent was built in 1846, the same year as the 'Works and Mills', whose entrance archway you will see on the left. **At the T-junction with Wharfdale Road, cross over and turn right. Take the first left into New Wharf Road.**

Shortly you will come across the London Canal Museum, located in Carlo Gatti's old ice warehouse. Exhibits include a bargee's living quarters (cramped but quaint), and a deep ice-storage pit, used for huge quantities of ice that were imported from Norway. If canal transport interests you, there is also an extensive range of books, maps etc. for sale. Open 10:00-16:30 Tuesday to Sunday, last entry 15:45.

Turn right into All Saint's Street, soon meeting the Caledonian Road. Turn left here to **cross the Regent's Canal.**

To the right you will see the canal entrance to Islington Tunnel, 960 yards long and opened in 1816. There is no towpath through the tunnel, so the bargeman had to 'leg' the boat through, lying on his back with his feet 'walking' along the tunnel walls. This exhausting method continued for 10 years until a towing boat was introduced.

Use the first crossing you come to and continue north, passing Copenhagen Street. Just after the Cally Pool on the left, turn right to follow

Richmond Avenue. **Take the first left into Matilda Street,** cross to the right-hand pavement, and continue around the perimeter of Thornhill Square, with the gardens on your left.

Notice the variety of coal-hole lids here, with four or five different makers, including a posh sunburst design from Clark, Hunt & Co., Shoreditch.

At the junction with Bridgeman Road, with St Andrew's Church on the left, turn right and then shortly left to follow Hemingford Road. Continue over the roundabout into Roman Way (Caledonian Road and Barnsbury station is to the left here).

You are now in Barnsbury, a fashionable residential district with good, solid, mostly well-kept Victorian family houses. At the roundabout junction with Offord Road is a pub that looks more like a vertical garden, its name completely obscured by greenery. This is the Hemingford Arms, where customers can enjoy food and real ale while seated amongst a cosy jumble of ephemera. A little further on is the Roman café/bistro, a good spot for a tea break.

Continue along Roman Way, crossing the North London line, and then take the first left, Wheelwright Street. Continue downhill to make acquaintance once more with Caledonian Road. Cross at the crossing and **turn right, with the massive bulk of Pentonville Prison for company on your right.** Carry on uphill, and when eventually the road levels out, at the Methodist Church **turn left to follow Market Road.** Soon you will come to Caledonian Park on your right. **Go through a gate into the park, and follow a path (or cut across the grass) to the clock tower.**

Fixed to the Portland stone buttress of this imposing timepiece is a plaque that announces: 'Copenhagen

Above and left: Thornhill Square exhibits an interesting selection of coal-hole lids

House, Famous tavern and tea garden stood here from early 17c. to 1855. Caledonian Market held here from 1870s until 1939. London Borough of Islington'.

The origins of this market lie in a long-overdue decision to move the live animal market here from Smithfield, for centuries the final destination for thousands of cattle, sheep, pigs, geese etc. that would arrive, driven from all parts of the country. Drunken drovers, rampaging animals and all the sights, smells and sounds of this open-air abattoir were finally too much for the City Corporation, who in 1855 opened the Caledonian Market on this site. On Mondays and Thursdays the cattle market was held, and on Tuesdays and Fridays a general market.

Above: The clock tower in Caledonian Park

Ward, Lock's London guide book of 1938, printed one year before the market closed permanently, mentions that 'it is no uncommon sight to see 30,000 animals of one kind or another in the pens on a single day'.

Friday was the day for the 'pedlar's market', when 'the variety of wares exposed for sale is extraordinary, and the crowd of buyers and spectators hardly less so'. The market did not re-open after the war, but the antique and flea-market re-established itself at Tower Bridge Road, Bermondsey.

Keep on along the path to rejoin Market Road through the solid but battered iron railings, and turn right. **At the T-junction with York Way use the crossing and then turn right, uphill. Bear left to follow Camden Park Road for 100 yards then right to follow Cliff Villas.** At the T-junction **turn right into Cliff Road, then at York Way turn left** (there are shops here for basic needs). **After 50 yards go left through a little arch into Camden Mews.** Follow the mews ahead (to avoid the uneven surface, continue to Camden Road and turn left for a parallel route).

Above: Stepping back in time in Camden Mews

On your right is a rustic removals warehouse offering 'Covered Vans from 1/6d per hour'. What a bargain! This long, straight, cobbled mews contains an eclectic mix of buildings, old and new. It provides a pleasurable downhill stroll for half a mile or so.

Cross Camden Park Road with care, diverting right to the traffic lights if necessary. After crossing two more roads, when Camden Mews comes to an end, **turn left into Rochester Square, then immediately right down a path in front of a terrace of houses** with neat ironwork and balconies. **Cross the next road and turn right, then left into Camden Road.** Continue past Camden Road station, soon crossing the canal again.

At pedestrian lights by a supermarket, cross then turn left and weave your way through the increasing throngs of people until you **cross Kentish Town Road and meet Camden High Street**. There are old-style, subterranean toilets in the middle of this road junction. **Turn right up Camden High Street**, and jostle your way through the crowds of pleasure-seekers, to finally **arrive at Camden Lock, on the Regent's Canal.**

Camden Lock Market is amazing. Small, individual shops sell an extraordinary selection of clothes, leather goods, books, furniture, every conceivable item of adornment for house and home, and every type of food imaginable. Exotic sights, sounds, and aromas stimulate the senses as you wander round, trying to take it all in. Next door, the Stables Market, cobbled and crowded, proclaims its status as the largest market in Camden, with 450 shops.

This unique interchange of road, rail, and canal, which until 1971 was a hard working timber wharf, might not exist now if plans for a motorway in the 1960s had come to fruition. The scheme involved demolishing the old

Left: The Regent's Canal at Camden Lock

buildings and filling in the canal, but thankfully intense local pressure finally put paid to these plans and in 1973 the market opened, with designers and artisans quick to move in. Another battle has recently been won; to save a network of horse-tunnels, built underground to facilitate transfer of goods from canal to railway, from being blocked by a housing development. Horses were the canal's motive power, hence the extensive stables.

This 21st-century 'pleasure ground' is your final destination, where you can enjoy a stroll along the canal towpath, a visit to the adjacent market, or maybe indulge in the abundance of refreshments on offer. Vauxhall now seems but a distant memory, a different world. Well done.

5 A Taste of Eastern Markets

Walthamstow to Petticoat Lane in two stages

Several renowned markets are featured on this walk through east London. Walthamstow's mile-long High Street of stalls, reputed to be the longest street market in Europe, provides a lively prelude to visiting two or three smaller, individual market sites. Then, by way of the peaceful Lea Valley and bustling Hackney, the walk hurries on to the 'Curry Capital' of east London at Brick Lane, before becoming immersed in a crush of bargain-hunters at Middlesex Street, known to one and all as 'Petticoat Lane'.

All the markets mentioned here are very popular, but Brick Lane, Spitalfields, and Petticoat Lane almost burst at the seams on a Sunday. One option is to set aside a weekend to walk from Walthamstow to Broadway Market on Saturday, then from Columbia Road to Petticoat Lane for a Sunday morning treat. This way you will see all the markets in full swing. If you would rather avoid the crowds, go on a weekday; it's still an excellent walk.

The markets are open at the following times:

Walthamstow High Street Stalls here all weekdays, busiest on Saturday.

Broadway Market Saturday only.

Columbia Road Flower Market Sunday 08:00 to 14:00.

Brick Lane and Cheshire Street Sunday 08:00 to 14:00.

Old Spitalfields Market Monday–Friday 10:00 to 14:00, Sunday 09:00 to 17:00.

Petticoat Lane Stalls in nearby Wentworth Street Monday–Friday 10:00 to 14:00. The main market, in Middlesex Street and surrounding streets, is held on Sunday from 09:00 to14:00.

Stage One: Walthamstow to Hackney

Distance 5 ½ miles. Intermediate distances: Walthamstow Library 1 mile, Coppermill Lane 2 miles, Springfield Marina 3 miles, Lea Bridge 4 miles.

Time 3 hours.

Terrain Paved and fairly level throughout, except for a gravel path beside the River Lea, which is crossed by a stepped footbridge.

Refreshments You are spoilt for choice in Walthamstow, and again in Hackney. There is a café at Springfield Marina, and two pubs at Lea Bridge. If the weather is kind, there are several pleasant picnic spots and shaded park benches, along with pavement cafés and plenty of pubs. Jellied eels and pie and mash are on the menu at Manze's in Walthamstow High Street, opposite which is Café Rio, complete with startling décor.

Toilets Walthamstow bus station and Library, Hackney Library and Mare Street.

Transport Fare zones 2 & 3. Walthamstow Central (train, Tube, bus), Walthamstow Queen's Road, and St James' Street (train, bus), Clapton (train, bus), Hackney Central and Hackney Downs (train, bus).

Best time to do the walk For the markets, Saturday. For an invigorating stride, anytime.

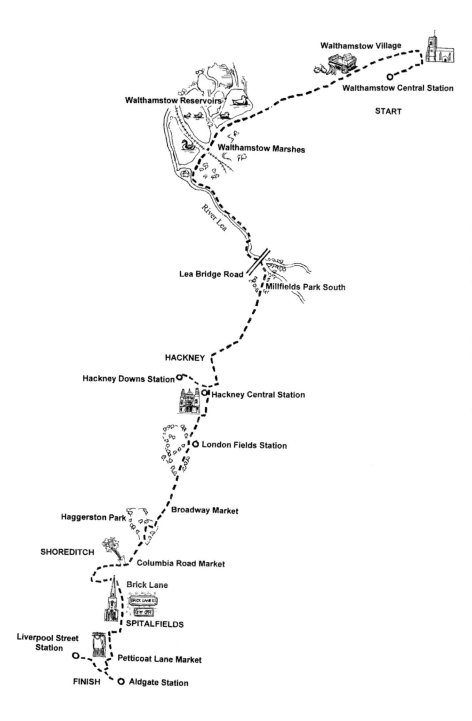

Walthamstow Village

Walthamstow Central Station

START

Walthamstow Reservoirs

Walthamstow Marshes

River Lea

Lea Bridge Road

Millfields Park South

HACKNEY

Hackney Downs Station

Hackney Central Station

London Fields Station

Broadway Market

Haggerston Park

SHOREDITCH

Columbia Road Market

Brick Lane

BRICK LANE E1

Liverpool Street Station

SPITALFIELDS

Petticoat Lane Market

FINISH

Aldgate Station

The probable Old English meaning of 'Wilcomestou', as Walthamstow used to be called, is 'a place where strangers are welcome'. Certainly the area is home to an extraordinary mix of cultures, evident as long ago as the 12th century when Ralph de Toni, a Norman nobleman, became lord of the manor through marriage. Family trees of the various holders of this position over the centuries are on show in a beautifully illustrated display contained in the Old Library, which you will pass later on. Two notables mentioned in this display are Joffre The Hairy, and, some years on, Baldwin The Bald.

Start at Walthamstow Central station (and bus station) in Selborne Road (Victoria line, trains to Liverpool Street). Walk the few yards to The Goose pub and **cross Hoe Street at the traffic lights to go straight ahead on St Mary Road.** At the end of this road continue ahead on Church Path, passing a pleasantly rustic row of cottages. Shortly you will emerge at Church End.

This is the peaceful and historic village centre of Walthamstow. On your right is the Vestry House Museum, which contains an absorbing record of local life, people, and industry through the ages, including the locally built Bremer car, the first British car with an internal combustion engine, dating from 1892. This neat little vehicle, which boasts spoon brakes and tiller steering, was reckoned to have a maximum safe speed of 7–8 miles per hour when it completed the Brighton Run in 1965, after breaking down the year before. Sitting incongruously on the grass verge outside the museum entrance is a massive Ionic stone capital, part of one of the columns from the portico of the Old General Post Office at St Martin-le-Grand which was bought by a local stone mason when the building was demolished. It arrived here in 1954.

Above: A sign on the wall of the Vestry House

Opposite the museum is the former St Mary's National

School, built in 1819, and adjacent to this, the diminutive Old Fire Station. On the left are Squires Almshouses, erected in 1795 'for the use of Six Decayed Tradesmens Widows of This Parish and No Other'. Decayed in those days meant you were really on your uppers, penniless.

Right: The Vestry House Museum, Walthamstow Village

Keep ahead for 50 yards to a red Victorian pillar-box by the churchyard, with Orford Road opposite. If time permits, a detour of a few minutes to the cafés, pubs, and Old Town Hall in Orford Road is a good idea.

Here on the corner is The Ancient House, a handsome, rebuilt timber-framed 15th-century dwelling, still lived in. To your left is St Mary's Church, a coating of cement render disguising the building's great age. The first permanent church was established here in the 12th century, probably by Ralph de Toni, and there are memorials inside going back as far as the 15th century. From this later period, on the north-west buttress of the tower, there is an inconspicuous, dinner-plate size carving of the 'Agnes Dei', or Lamb of God.

Turn left, through the churchyard, and go past the church.

Glance to your right to admire the 16th-century Monoux Almshouses, partly rebuilt after wartime damage. George Monoux was a local resident and benefactor, who had made his fortune as a City merchant, and was twice Lord Mayor of London, in 1514 and 1528. Next to the almshouses is Vinegar Alley, thought to get its name from the vinegar used as disinfectant in a plague pit that was sited here.

Maintaining the same direction, leave the churchyard and go forward to the junction with Church Hill. Turn left, downhill, passing the Walthamstow School for Girls. Continue down Church Hill to the junction with Hoe Street.

If Arts and Crafts design interests you, now is your chance to visit the William Morris Gallery in Forest Road, housed in a handsome old building that served as the Morris family home from 1848–56.

Optional Diversion to the William Morris Gallery...

Turn right here to follow Hoe Street for ½ mile to Bell Corner, where you turn left into Forest Road. The gallery is on the right, in Lloyd Park (there is an automatic toilet near the park gates). Afterwards, retrace your steps to this point.

Continuing on the main walk...

Cross Hoe Street at the lights to keep going along High Street into the market area. Soon you will come to the part old, part new library.

Located on the first floor of the library, reached by a grand staircase, is the splendid family tree display mentioned earlier. There are toilets on the ground and first floors. Back on the High Street, you can't escape the costermongers bawling out today's bargains; 'three pound o' coxes a pound' 'strawberries a pound a punnet'. Kilograms and litres are not welcome here. A little more discreetly, from a stall glittering with shiny, cheap watches; 'quality watches, no problem, you bring back if no work, have another'. Quite a way along is Manze's eel, pie, and mash emporium, sporting its original 1929 tiled interior, and on the opposite side of the road is Café Rio, full of an extraordinary mixture of ephemera, including two old-style petrol pumps.

Right: Bargains galore in Walthamstow Market

Keep on ahead through the melee of the market, crossing first Willow Walk and later on St James's Street (turn left here for railway station and, just beyond, toilets). Now you are on Coppermill Lane, still maintaining the same direction. Pass Coppermill Park and The Coppermill pub. **Carry on straight ahead past the water treatment works and reservoir to a low railway bridge.**

Once past the rather intimidating barrier-like iron sculpture, 'Split-Leaf', where you cross the Lee flood relief channel, your arrival at number 5 of the Walthamstow Reservoirs is heralded not by the market trader's cries, but by the assorted calls of geese, ducks, coots, and all manner of wildfowl, as they take advantage of the safety of the reservoir's islands. A large colony of cormorants is resident, and amongst the complex of reservoirs (which have been in use since 1866) there is also an important heronry with up to 200 breeding

103

pairs. Little egrets, too, breed in small numbers here. Not surprisingly, with all these herons to feed, the reservoirs are well stocked with fish, and if a future visit appeals to you, day permits can be obtained for angling, birdwatching, or just walking the perimeter paths (these are available from the Fishery Centre in Ferry Lane, a ten minute walk from Tottenham Hale station.)

On your left are the extensive filter-beds of Coppermills water treatment works. All thought of the market bustle is now forgotten as you stroll down this quiet lane, passing under power lines. The Italianate building to your right is the old coppermill, which was converted to a waterworks pumping station in 1860. For over two hundred years before this there had been a mill on this site, producing in turn powder, paper, leather, linseed oil, and from 1808 to 1857, copper. In a while you arrive at a car park and entrance to Walthamstow Marsh Nature Reserve, a Site of Special Scientific Interest, and a place where water voles, edible frogs, bats and warblers share these ancient water meadows with an abundance of plants and flowers, some rare. Go past this to duck down under what is arguably London's lowest railway bridge.

Limbo under the 5 ft bridge and continue on a tarmac path beside the nature reserve. This curves to the right at Springfield Marina. **On the curve, turn left through a barrier to follow a gravel track signed for Lee Valley Ice Centre** (for the café, do not turn left, just carry on and cross the bridge ahead). Keep going until you arrive at the river.

Above: Better for cattle than humans–low bridge at Walthamstow Marsh

The River Lea (or Lee, the spelling used for the Navigation and man-made channels) rises near Luton and flows for 50 miles to meet the Thames at Canning Town. The Lee Valley Regional Park, all 10,000 acres of it, keeps company with the river for 26 miles of nature reserves, country parks and lakeside trails, with good access for walking and cycling. This short stretch provides a sample of London's second river.

On meeting the River Lea and Horseshoe Bridge, bear left to follow the riverside path (if you would like to visit the Anchor and Hope pub, a bit further down river on the opposite bank, cross the bridge and take the parallel route).

Above: Herons and cormorants have large nesting sites on the Walthamstow reservoirs

In July 1909, Walthamstow Marsh witnessed the first all-British powered aeroplane flight when A V Roe piloted his marvellous creation for 900 ft, skimming across the marsh at a height of 10 ft. The firm of AVRO went on to build Shackleton, Lancaster, and Vulcan bombers.

Carry on under the railway and, after ¼ mile, turn right to cross the iron footbridge over the Lea. Keep on along the riverside to go under Lea Bridge.

Here is a pleasant spot for a break, with the 'Ship Aground' and 'Princess of Wales' tempting you to stay, and Lea Bridge Weir plus the nearby park providing scenic appeal.

At this point you say goodbye to the London Borough of Waltham Forest and hallo to Hackney, the name probably derived from 'Hakon's- ey'; an 'ey' being a raised place in a marsh, or an island. Before the mid 1800s, Hackney was utterly different to what we see today. Set in pleasant countryside, but not too far from the city, it appealed to the rich; they built grand houses, and particularly schools, here. Samuel Pepys, who went to school in Hackney, visited here in April 1667, and noted in his diary: 'To Hackney church. A Knight and his lady very civil to me when they came, being Sir George Viner, and his lady in rich jewells, but most in beauty: almost the finest woman that ever I saw. That which I went chiefly to see was the young ladies of the schools, whereof there is great store, very pretty'.

The towpath takes you over an old dock entrance opposite the weir. Before a house and bridge turn right, away from the river, on a shared cycle and pedestrian path (signed for Clapton) across Millfields Park South. There are three cast-iron LCC borough boundary markers by the path. Walk the full length of this park to join Chatsworth Road, which you cross, and then go ahead, gently uphill, on Powerscroft Road. Make sure you stay on this road as it bears to the right at a Y-junction. **Soon you arrive at a T-junction with Lower Clapton Road.**

To your left is the Round Chapel, which was opened in 1871. At first known as the Clapton Park United Reformed Church, it was one of the most important non-conformist churches in east London. It possesses a spacious, theatre-like interior, the galleries and ceiling supported on slender cast-iron columns combined with delicate lattice-work arches. The worshippers have moved next door, and the building is now run by the Hackney Historic Buildings Trust. If you have two minutes to spare, turn right and right again into Linscott Road to see the extraordinary temple-like structure that was once The London Orphan Asylum.

Use the crossing to go down Clapton Passage, directly opposite. This leads to Clapton Square, where you continue ahead to turn left and follow the far side of the square.

Clapton Square was laid out in 1816, on a piece of open land known as Clapton Field, and these fashionable dwellings were then erected piecemeal, rather than as a planned development. . At number 13, Hackney's lord of the manor once had his office. The remaining original houses on the square's northern and western sides are much appreciated these days for their Georgian good looks.

At the end of the square turn left into Lower Clapton Road for 50 yards, cross at the zebra crossing, and continue ahead into Churchwell Path. Walk through a pleasant garden area to the porch of St John at Hackney church.

This huge church was built to accommodate a congregation of 2000; not bad on a budget of only £10,000. Designed by James Spiller and completed in 1797, it replaced an earlier church slightly to the west (St Augustine's), the 13th-century tower of which you will see in a moment. St John's eye-catching stone tower, which seems almost to be suspended, floating, above the church, was added fifteen years later. Clustered around the churchyard, orderly ranks of tombs contain some interesting individuals, including Conrad Loddiges (1738–1826), famous local nurseryman, who introduced wisteria and rhododendron, and whose customers included the Duke of Devonshire. By the 1820s his nursery was also offering a selection of over 1,000 tropical orchids for sale, grown in steam heated hothouses nearby. Near the information centre look out for Rear Admiral Sir Francis Beaufort's tomb, complete with full description of the Beaufort Wind Scale.

Go to the right, towards the back of the church, with a procession of tombs on your right. Bear half-right to follow a path through the churchyard, and at a junction of paths (by the Information Centre) turn right, signed for Mare Street.

You might like a brief diversion at this point, where a left turn will lead you along Sutton Place, at the end of which a right turn brings you, in a few steps, to 16th-century Sutton House. A National Trust property, Grade II listed, it is open Thursday-Sunday and Bank Holiday Mondays 12:00-16:30. On the way, look out for an unusual memorial, a small metal plaque to 'Blind Fred, a sunny soul', which has a Braille inscription.

At St Augustine's Tower bear left to then cross Mare Street at the crossing. Go ahead for 20 yards to cross Amhurst Road at the lights (a passageway here leads to Hackney Central station). Stage One finishes at this point, where you have the choice of catching a train on the North London line, which runs from Stratford to Richmond, from this station, or turning right to follow Amhurst Road to its junction with Dalston Lane, where a left turn will lead to Hackney Downs station for trains to Liverpool Street. There are plenty of buses from Mare Street to many east and north London destinations.

Left: One of the interesting occupants of St John-at-Hackney graveyard

Stage Two: Hackney to Petticoat Lane

Distance 3 ½ miles.
Intermediate distances: London
Fields ½ mile, Columbia Road
1½ miles, Brick Lane 2½ miles.

Time 2 hours.

Terrain Paved and reasonably
level all the way, some cobbles
to negotiate at Columbia Road.

Refreshments There is a wide
selection in Hackney, and several
places in Broadway Market,
including Cooke's pie and mash
emporium. Columbia Road has
one or two cafés, and there is a tea
stall by St Leonard's Church, in
Calvert Avenue, Shoreditch. Brick
Lane and Spitalfields are home
to every conceivable kind of re-
fuelling venue, with some quaint,
older establishments in Brushfield
Street and the surrounding streets.

Toilets Hackney Library and
Mare Street, London Fields,
Haggerston Park, Hackney Road/
Columbia Road, Middlesex Street.

Transport Fare zones 1 & 2.
Hackney Central and Hackney
Downs (train, bus), London Fields
(train), Cambridge Heath (train,
bus), Liverpool Street (train,
Tube, bus), Aldgate and Aldgate
East (Tube, bus). Shoreditch
station is closed until 2010.

Best time to do the walk
This stage is full of interest at any
time, but Columbia Road flower
market only opens on Sunday
mornings, which is also the time
to see Petticoat Lane at full stretch.

Right: Some well-
built statuary in
London Fields

Until Hackney was covered in bricks and mortar, there were fields, farms, and market gardens in abundance. The walk sets off to follow an old route along which produce was taken to feed London's hungry citizens.

Start at Hackney Central station (North London line, frequent buses). From Amhurst Road, go under the railway bridge and continue along Mare Street. **Cross Graham Road and pass the Hackney Empire and the Town Hall.**

The Empire was designed by famous theatre architect Frank Matcham and opened in 1901, after taking just 38 weeks to build. An audience up to 3,000 strong were entertained by acts from across the world including Charlie Chaplin, Marie Lloyd (who lived nearby), and in later years famous names such as Tony Hancock and Max Miller before fashions changed and the theatre closed in 1956. After serving time as the first commercial television studio in the country and then a bingo hall, a preservation trust was formed, and the

Left: The Hackney Empire sports an extravagant display of ornamentation

theatre re-opened in 1986. It is now enjoying great success, presenting comedy, drama, dance, opera, and concerts.

Just beyond the Town Hall is Hackney's Library and Museum, the latter containing a comprehensive display of local life, industry, and curiosities, including the Hackney Log Boat, which is over a thousand years old. It was discovered in Springfield Park near the River Lee in 1987 and is now safe under a thick glass floor. There are toilets in the museum and at first floor level in the library.

Turn right in front of the library (in Reading Lane) **and immediately left into Hackney Grove,** the old route to London's markets, where the footpath again runs alongside a cycle track. Your route now runs arrow-straight, in company with the cycle track, along Hackney Grove, then Martello Street, under the railway bridge and past the Pub on the Park (with London Fields station adjacent), and then through a gate (toilets here), to follow London Fields' tree-shaded avenue and cycle track, at the end of which **cross Westgate Street and continue ahead through Broadway Market.**

Right: Saturday is the time to enjoy Broadway Market's tempting selection

111

Between the Cat and Mutton pub and the bridge over the Regent's Canal, this street is a reminder of how shopping used to be: small, independent shops where purchasing is a pleasure. A photograph taken in 1906 shows similarities with the scene today, albeit with different trades: at number 81, J Bassett & Son, Funeral Directors, 'Coffins in Lead, Oak and Elm' and next door G. Keagle, 'Feather dyer, Ostrich feathers'. Visit if you can on a Saturday, when an unhurried and homely farmers-cum-general market fills the street. For refreshment, most tastes are catered for, from a pub lunch to pie and mash or jellied eels. The Dove freehouse has wood-panelling, bags of character, offers 'London's finest selection of Belgian beers', and serves food.

The 8½ mile long Regent's Canal was opened in 1820 to link London's docks and wharves to the main Grand Union canal network. It runs from Little Venice, near Paddington, through inner north and east London, to Limehouse where it meets the Thames.

Left: Acton's Lock on the Regent's Canal at Haggerston

If you wish to leave the walk at this point, one option is to turn left into Andrews Road, which runs parallel to the canal (you will also see a notice proclaiming 'Regent's Canal via steps'), where a quarter-mile saunter along road or towpath, passing the huge gasholders on the other bank, will bring you to Mare Street. Buses from here run to Liverpool Street, Hackney, Blackfriars, Aldwych, and Waterloo.

At the traffic lights maintain the same direction, now on Goldsmith's Row. Soon you come to Haggerston Park, which you enter through a gate on the right. **Follow the woodland path,** bearing right, to arrive at a high brick wall. Turn left and after 60 yards (straight ahead for toilets) left again on a broad avenue, passing sports pitches on the right, and Hackney City Farm on the left. **Cross Hackney Road at lights to go ahead for a few yards and then right, along cobbled Columbia Road**.

Right: You have to be quick to get the best bargains in Columbia Road

A haven of calm during the week, enhanced by its charming, individual, wooden-shuttered little shops, Columbia Road assumes a different personality on Sunday mornings. This is when the flower market is held, an absolute riot of colour, fragrance, and tremendous bargains in flowers, plants, and shrubs.

Continue along Columbia Road, crossing Gosset Street at a mini roundabout, to the junction with Hackney Road (there is an automatic toilet here, located next to the red phone box). Now **turn left, and you will shortly arrive at Shoreditch High Street,** and St Leonard's Church.

This is the third church on this site, the first having been erected here in the 9th century. The predecessor of the present church dated from the 13th century, and was known as 'The Actor's Church', because so many of that profession were buried in the churchyard, Shoreditch having been home to England's first play-house, 'The Theatre', built by James Burbage in 1576. By the early 1700s this dilapidated medieval church was crumbling, with bits falling off during services. The church you see today, which opened in 1740, was designed by George Dance the Elder, architect of the Mansion House. It featured in the nursery rhyme 'Oranges and Lemons'; 'When I am rich, say the bells of Shoreditch'.

Pass the church and take the first left into Calvert Avenue. Continue to Arnold Circus, turn left, then take the second left into Palissy Street.

Old Nichol Slum, a notorious 'rookery', blighted this overcrowded area until it was demolished and replaced in the 1890s with these solid blocks of flats, known as the Boundary Street Estate. This was an early attempt by the newly created London County Council to improve conditions for the working classes, and included workshops for local craftsmen. The raised gardens and bandstand were created on top of a pile of rubble from the demolition.

At the T-junction with Swanfield Street turn right and immediately left into Brick Lane. Follow round a right-hand bend and then continue ahead on Brick Lane, crossing Bethnal Green Road at lights. You will soon arrive at the old Black Eagle Brewery of Truman, Hanbury and Buxton.

Truman's brewed beer on this site from the 17th century until closure of the brewery in 1989; now these noble old buildings are home to designer shops and a Sunday market. From here onwards you are in 'Banglatown', full of colour and curry-houses, and home to the largest Bengali community in the U.K. This area of the East End has sheltered immigrants for centuries; Huguenots in the 18th century, Jews in the 19th century, and in recent years Bangladeshis, have all sought a better life here. Brick Lane derived its name from clay-pits and brick-kilns sited here in days gone by, which provided thousands of bricks to help with the rebuilding of the City after the Great Fire of 1666.

Continue along Brick Lane past the brewery buildings and then turn right into Hanbury Street. Take the first left into Wilkes Street.

Right: Wilkes Street is at the heart of 18th-century Spitalfields

Comedian Bud Flanagan, leader of the Crazy Gang, is remembered with a blue plaque at number 12 Hanbury Street. He lived from 1896 to 1968. Long before then, Huguenot silk weavers, driven from France by religious persecution from 1683 onwards, occupied this area. They built these fine, plain, early 18th-century houses, some with weaver's windows in the roof, which help to give Spitalfields its unique character. It is possible to see inside a few of the original houses during London Open House weekend in September, but you may have to queue. As you walk along Wilkes Street look for Princelet Street, where at number 19 is a former silk weaver's home built in 1719, with a synagogue added at the rear in 1869.

Take the first right turn off Wilkes Street into paved Puma Court, where on the right are almshouses erected in 1860 for 'poor inhabitants in the liberty of Norton Folgate'. At the end **turn left into Commercial Street** for a few yards, and at the Ten Bells pub **cross at the pedestrian lights towards Old Spitalfields Market and turn left.**

King Charles II granted the first charter for a market here in 1682, and it's still going strong today. Although the fruit and vegetable wholesalers for whom it was originally built have gone to a new market site at Temple Mills, these unique buildings still host a wide variety of specialist stalls.

Below: Christ Church, Spitalfields

Look across the road to Christ Church, Spitalfields, now restored and open after years of decay. Designed by Nicholas Hawksmoor, and consecrated in 1729, it was one of six London churches that he built, provided for by the Fifty New Churches Act of 1711. This church-building spree had a purpose, which was to quell dissent and non-conformism, so the church buildings had to make a bold, no-nonsense statement. Christ Church certainly does that.

Cross Brushfield Street and, leaving Commercial Street, go **straight ahead into Toynbee Street,** passing White's Row. Take the next **right into Brune Street.**

As you walk along this quiet back street you will see on the right a terracotta façade announcing the 'Soup Kitchen for the Jewish Poor', and a few yards further on the name 'Tenter Ground' where cloth was hung on tenter frames to dry and stretch, 'on tenter hooks'.

At the end of Brune Street **turn left into Bell Lane.** Pass Cobb Street, **then turn next right** to wade through the sea of clothes on the market stalls of Wentworth Street.

Above: A quiet moment's trading near Petticoat Lane

You are now in the heart of 400-year-old Petticoat Lane Market, once a place to buy second-hand clothes, now a major tourist attraction. Re-named Middlesex Street by the Victorians, who didn't like to mention ladies' underwear, it is still Petticoat Lane to one and all.

Experience the crowds, colour, and banter on a Sunday, or take the opportunity on any other day of the week to explore the lanes, alleys, and side-streets that give this place such character, and make it enduringly popular with generations of bargain-hunters.

Shortly you will arrive at Middlesex Street, where the walk comes to an end. Turn right for Liverpool Street station and Bishopsgate, or left for Aldgate.

6 Secrets of Southwark

A circular tour from London Bridge to Rotherhithe and back in two stages

This round trip first visits Bankside and The Borough, areas just south of London Bridge that are crammed with the evidence of a thousand years of history, before moving on to Walworth, once described as '... the birthplace of the Cockney...homeland to the costers and pearlies'. From here the walk takes you to Bermondsey and Southwark Park, soon arriving at the reclaimed, watery world of the former Surrey Commercial Docks, where the teeming riverbank activity of olden times has virtually disappeared, but not without leaving its mark. Your return journey enjoys breathtaking riverside views, complemented by the old warehouses, inns, and red-brick 18th-century church that together make up Rotherhithe 'village'.

Stage One: London Bridge to Surrey Quays

Distance 5½ miles. Intermediate distances: St George's Church 1 mile, Walworth 2 miles, Merrow Street 3 miles, Thorburn Square 4 miles, Southwark Park 5 miles.

Time 3 hours.

Terrain Nearly all level and paved, except for a cobbled street at Bankside.

Refreshments Plenty of variety in Borough; a sprinkling of places at Walworth, Old Kent Road and Southwark Park Road.

Toilets London Bridge station, Borough Market, Elephant and Castle, Cuming Museum at Walworth, Southwark Park.

Transport Fare zones 1 & 2. London Bridge (Tube, train, bus), Borough (Tube, bus), Elephant and Castle (Tube, train, bus), South Bermondsey (train, bus), Canada Water (Tube, bus).

Best time to do the walk During the working week, or Saturday, when the markets, shops, and cafés are all open.

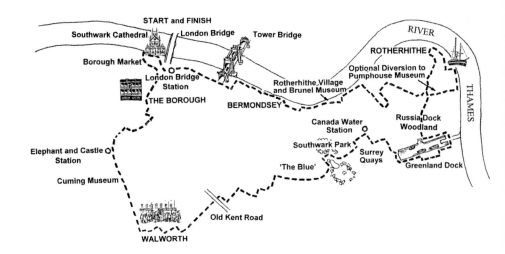

START and FINISH

Southwark Cathedral   London Bridge   Tower Bridge

RIVER

ROTHERHITHE

Borough Market

London Bridge Station

Optional Diversion to
Pumphouse Museum

Rotherhithe Village
and Brunel Museum

THE BOROUGH

BERMONDSEY

THAMES

Canada Water
Station

Russia Dock
Woodland

Elephant and Castle
Station

Southwark Park

Surrey
Quays

Cuming Museum

'The Blue'

Greenland Dock

Old Kent Road

WALWORTH

Right: A relief
depiction of the Surrey
Commercial Docks tops
the summit of Stave Hill

Borough High Street's ribbon of inns and alehouses has offered entertainment and hospitality for centuries. Being outside the City's somewhat puritanical jurisdiction, Bankside, offering brothels, bear-baiting, and all manner of bawdy attractions, served as London's stress-reliever. Present day pleasure-seekers still flock to Southwark's various historic and modern delights, but tend to be a little less rowdy than their uninhibited ancestors.

Start at London Bridge station (Northern and Jubilee lines, trains from Charing Cross, Waterloo East, Lewisham, East Croydon) and **make your way to Borough High Street, which you cross at the lights at St Thomas Street to follow Bedale Street**, which is opposite. Walk through the stalls and shops of Borough Market to continue ahead on Cathedral Street.

An informal produce market had been operating, chaotically, along the road to the Great Stone Gate

Left: Tantalizing displays in Borough Market are hard to resist

at the southern end of London Bridge for centuries before an Act of Parliament created Borough Market in its present, more suitable location in 1756. This bustling, colourful venue with its well-stocked stalls is still a magnet for food lovers 250 years later. Tempting stacks of organic fruit and vegetables, cheese, bread, and meat surround you, making it unlikely that you will leave here without a bag of something delicious. No wonder it is known as 'London's Larder'.

You are now at the western end of Southwark Cathedral. **Bear left towards St Mary Overie's Dock, and the Golden Hinde.**

Southwark Cathedral was built on an already sacred site. The Augustinian Priory of St Mary Overie ('over the river') was established here in 1106, burnt to the ground in 1212, rebuilt, and then closed by Henry VIII at the Reformation. As if this wasn't enough to cope with, hard times caused parts of St Saviour's Parish Church, as it then was, to be let out as a bakery, pottery, and even a pig-sty. In the 17th century the church was bought by its parishioners, and elevation to the role of Cathedral in 1905 has helped to preserve this beautiful Gothic building. Inside, there are many fascinating memorials, including a carved figure of William Shakespeare in front of a scene of Bankside as it was in his day. His brother Edmund is buried here. John Harvard, the man who endowed Harvard University, is remembered in the Harvard Chapel, after his baptism here in 1607. Even if you don't have time now, a future visit is well worth a special trip.

Above: Safe in its own little dock, the Golden Hinde adds to Bankside's unique appeal

Opposite the gangplank of the Golden Hinde, by the Old Thameside Inn, **continue into Clink Street** at Pickfords Wharf.

This colourful replica of Sir Francis Drake's galleon has itself circumnavigated the globe. It is quite startling, but exciting, to come across this impressive ship in a little dock, hemmed in by old buildings. An information board tells you all about it. Open 7 days 10:00–17:30.

Carry on along Clink Street, past the remains of Winchester Palace.

The Bishop of Winchester's palace was right next to a den of raucous entertainments which included the 'stews' (brothels) where the ladies were known as 'Winchester Geese'. This area was the 'Liberty of the Clink' although liberty was something that the next door Clink Prison's inmates did not enjoy. Some had to rely on begging through a pavement grille to avoid starvation. The Clink Prison Museum is captivating, but beware; it is also very realistic. Open 7 days 10:00–18:00.

Pass the Clink Prison Museum, go under the railway bridge, and at Vinopolis turn immediately left into Park Street (on the right is the historic Anchor Inn, where you can enjoy a drink by the river). Follow Park Street straight ahead (not right) back to the market at Stoney Street, then **turn right to Southwark Street**, where you go right for a few steps to the Hop Exchange.

It used to be said that you could tell your whereabouts in this part of the world by the smell; the heavy aroma of hops in The Borough, or a sometimes nauseous reek

Left: A magnificent façade announces the Hop Exchange

of tanneries in Bermondsey. Here you can still see the magnificent Hop Exchange, dating from 1866. Just peep through the glass doors to a galleried interior where hops from Kent, Hereford, and Worcester were traded with the benefit of natural light from the building's glass roof. No wonder this was a busy place; there were numerous inns hereabouts, whose customers no doubt consumed prodigious quantities of beer, brewed locally by Barclay Perkins, and Courage.

Retrace your few steps and cross Southwark Street at the central iron-grilled refuge to a side road opposite, which is part of Borough High Street. Go down here for 50 yards.

On the right, in a private courtyard (Calvert's Buildings), can be seen a half-timbered house with overhanging upper floor, a survivor of a devastating fire in Southwark in 1676. Over 100 years before, around 1540, this had been the Goat Inn.

From here, **turn around to pass to the right of the War Memorial, walk forward along Borough High Street for 70 yards, and cross to the right at the lights.** If you would like to view the 18th-century quadrangle of Guy's Hospital, or visit the Old Operating Theatre Museum and Herb Garret, turn left, then right into St Thomas Street where you will find them close by. Otherwise, **turn right to go south along Borough High Street.**

All the old coaching inns were here, their names recalled in the narrow yards leading off; King's Head Yard (a 17th-century bust of Henry VIII is on display on the Victorian pub here); White Hart Yard, George Inn Yard, Talbot Yard, Queen's Head Yard. Before the railways arrived, over 140 stage-coaches left from here every week, bound for the southern counties. Now only the 17th-century George Inn (or part of it) remains, the north and central parts having been demolished in 1889 by its owner, the Great Northern Railway. It's worth going in for a quick drink, to step

Left: Borough High Street's famous galleried George Inn

back in time 300 years. Look out for 'WH & H LeMay, Hop Factors', ornate terracotta façade at number 67. There are also several 'Historic Southwark' plaques dotted about on walls and in courtyards, helping to fill in some historical details.

From the famous Tabard Inn (now gone, and its yard renamed Talbot) Chaucer's pilgrims set off for Canterbury in April 1386. They would have followed Kent (now Tabard) Street, which traces the line of Watling Street, the Roman road to Dover.

At Newcomen Street, a brief digression to the King's Arms will reveal a richly carved Royal Coat of Arms, dated 1760, which was previously on Old London Bridge's gatehouse.

Continue along Borough High Street, passing several old courtyards where an emerging coach and four would not look out of place.

Across the road is Little Dorrit Park, and in front of you is Little Dorrit's church, St George the Martyr, with a representation of her in the modern east window. There has been a church at this important road junction since at least the 12th century, while the building that you see today dates from 1736. In Charles Dickens's tale of Little Dorrit, written in 1856, she lived with her parents in the Marshalsea Prison, just across the road from the church, and on returning home late one night and finding herself locked out, she slept in the vestry, with just the church register for a pillow. Charles Dickens knew this area well, having lodged in nearby Lant Street while his father was confined in Marshalsea Prison for debt. At that time, The Borough had more than its fair share of prisons, cheek by jowl with the inns and ale-houses. One wall of the prison remains, between St George's churchyard and Angel Place. Weller Street, Pickwick Street, and other Dickensian names adorn several local streets, and there is a Charles Dickens school (and pub) nearby.

Cross Tabard Street, pass St George's Church, then cross Great Dover Street, into which you then turn left, and then take the first right into Swan Street. Shortly Trinity Street crosses; turn left here to arrive at Trinity Church Square.

This tranquil late Georgian square is at the heart of a 24 acre estate owned by Trinity House, the rents from which are used for the benefit of poor seafarers in old age, sickness or distress. Holy Trinity Church, as it was, is now Henry Wood Hall, a grand venue for orchestral rehearsals.

Safe behind railings, the statue of King Alfred stands enigmatically, watching the world change as the centuries pass. Known as London's oldest outdoor statue, it is believed to date from the 14th century, and was previously sited at Westminster Hall. It was placed here when this area was being developed around 1820–30.

After passing the statue, turn right to follow the perimeter of the square, and then turn left into Brockham Street. This will take you to Harper Road, which you cross to **go through**

a gate into Newington Gardens. Bear half-right to leave the park by a children's playground, then **carry on ahead on Avonmouth Street.**

The long arm of the law makes itself felt here, for on your right is the Inner London Crown Court, while Newington Gardens sprang from the site of Horsemonger Lane Gaol, where the unsavoury spectacle of public hangings, carried out on the roof, continued until the 1860s.

Avonmouth Street meets Newington Causeway. Turn left here, go under the railway bridge, and just before the roundabout look for a ramp which you follow down to go through a subway heading towards Elephant and Castle Shopping Centre. Emerging on the far side, turn right up a ramp to pass the Underground station entrance and the step-free access to the shopping centre, which has one or two cafés, and toilets on the first floor. Keep ahead to the end of the shopping centre, and then **go left into Walworth Road.**

Opposite this worldly place of bustle, bus stops and market stalls is the Metropolitan Tabernacle, built for C H Spurgeon, a 19th-century Baptist preacher whose compelling sermons were so good that he could fill this giant edifice to its 6,000 person capacity, with more eager worshippers pressing at the doors.

Carry on down Walworth Road, passing the giant housing blocks of the Heygate Estate, the Cuming Museum, and East Street Market.

Right: Fine Georgian houses take pride of place in Surrey Square

The Cuming Museum is much too good to pass by without visiting, so why not have a break from walking and be entertained by an extraordinary range of exhibits, including such treasures as a Maori nose-flute, an ancient stuffed bear, a mask from an Egyptian mummy, and a bespangled jacket belonging to Tommy Johnson MBE, Pearly King of Bankside and

Bow Bells. There are regular temporary exhibitions, often focusing on the local area. The museum is open Tuesday-Saturday 10:00-17:00, admission free. Further on, East Street Market displays a less esoteric selection of goods, and when the market is in full swing, you can buy a pair of shoes for a fiver, a suit for twenty pounds, pawn your watch or even treat yourself to some jellied eels

After passing Marks and Spencer, take the second turning on the left into Liverpool Grove, and continue past St Peter's Church to bear right past a row of quaint cottages. **At Portland Street, turn right, then left into Merrow Street.**

Designed by Sir John Soane and completed by 1825, yellow-brick St Peter's is a pleasure to behold. Built as one of the 'Waterloo Churches', in celebration of victory over Napoleon, it was badly damaged in the last war, but is now splendidly restored. Once past the church and old cottages you enter an estate planned in 1904 by Octavia Hill, a founder of The National Trust and housing reformer. These low-rise flats and houses have an air of quality and permanence quite unmatched by more recent social housing nearby.

Cross Villa Street and keep going until Merrow Street ends at Dawes Street. Here **turn right** on a side road to **then turn left** after a few yards **at Inville Road,** between the bulky slab blocks of the Aylesbury Estate. **Cross Thurlow Street** and carry on ahead under an arch, **now on Alsace Road. Follow this into Surrey Square,** passing a terrace of Georgian houses. **Cross the Old Kent Road to continue ahead on Penry Street.**

Turn right into Marcia Road, at the end of which you **turn left into Dunton Road,** opposite a supermarket car park.

Cross Mandela Way and after 100 yards take the first right, Lynton Road. Now take the third turning on the left, Reverdy Road. Turn first right into Fort Road, which leads you through an archway **to Thorburn Square,** and go to the left of St Anne's Church, through another archway, to **follow Longley Street. At Southwark Park Road turn right, and continue past the Queen Victoria pub to cross St James's Road** at the lights and keep going into the market and shops of 'The Blue'.

Left: The Blue Market evokes memories of busier times in Southwark Park Road

No doubt the neat little Victorian cottages you have just passed would be worth a fortune in Chelsea, but this area is still waiting to be discovered. Southwark Park Road is home to the unpretentious 'village' called 'The Blue'; hence the Blue Market, Blue Anchor pub, and even a blue painted railway bridge. Before supermarkets existed, Blue Anchor Road (as it was then called), contained a tumult of shopping activity among its numerous market stalls. Trade may not be quite so brisk now, but there is still a down-to-earth feel of a bit of old Bermondsey here. Look out for Lou Farrow's café, where pie, mash and liquor costs less than a supermarket sandwich.

For South Bermondsey station (trains to London Bridge) **turn right at Galleywall Road** and continue to its end, opposite which is the station entrance.

To continue on the walk route, where the shops thin out, use the crossing to gain the left-hand pavement. Carry on ahead **through a tunnel under the railway, cross Drummond Road, and continue along Southwark Park Road**, which curves to the left. At Southwark Park Primary School, cross the road to **enter Jamaica Gate into Southwark Park,** and follow the road ahead.

This leafy, verdant interlude is a good antidote to all the tarmac-tramping that you have just done, and also a pleasing prelude to the second stage of the Secrets of Southwark walk, which is quite unlike the first.

Carry on ahead through the park on a wide road that soon curves to the right. Shortly you will see a small but welcoming café (with toilets).

Below: A sundial proclaims 1936 as the year of the creation of Ada Salter Gardens

To your right are the Ada Salter Gardens, created in 1936 and named after the wife of Dr Alfred Salter, local councillor and MP. Fragrant floral beds, a lake full of birdlife and a wrought-iron sundial complement this tranquil spot.

After a break here, **bear left and leave the park through a grand set of gates** leading to Gomm Road.

129

Carry on along this road, passing a neat terrace of bay-windowed cottages.

The plaque at number 36 mentions Richard Carr-Gomm, social reformer and founder of two housing societies, and a member of an important local family who were at one time lords of the manor of Rotherhithe.

At the end of Gomm Road turn left and then cross to the right at the lights to follow Surrey Quays Road for 250 yards, passing the restored Dock Offices, to arrive at Canada Water station, and the end of Stage One of 'Secrets of Southwark'.

Left: Deal porters forever at work beside Canada Water

Stage Two: Surrey Quays to London Bridge

Distance 5 miles. Intermediate distances: Rainbow Quay 1 mile, Stave Hill 2 miles, Rotherhithe Village 3 miles, St Saviour's Dock 4 miles.

Time 3 hours.

Terrain Mostly level tarmac or pavement, but with some uneven surfaces and cobblestones.

Refreshments Surrey Quays, the Moby Dick at Greenland Dock, Mayflower, Ship, and Angel inns at Rotherhithe, cafés and pubs in Tower Bridge Road, Tooley Street, Borough Market and Borough High Street at walk's end.

Toilets Canada Water, Surrey Quays Shopping Centre, Tooley Street, London Bridge station.

Transport Fare zones 1 & 2. Canada Water (Tube, bus), Bermondsey (Tube, bus), London Bridge (Tube, train, bus).

Best time to do the walk Monday to Friday, to visit the fascinating Pumphouse Museum.

Right: At the entrance to Greenland Dock, a capstan is framed by the distant towers of Canary Wharf

Start at Canada Water station, on the Jubilee line. **Turn left into Deal Porters Way** towards Surrey Quays Shopping Centre, passing a bronze and timber representation, amongst the reeds, of some deal porters at their back-breaking work unloading timber. Pass a viewing platform and when you come to the water's end curve left and then right to carry on past the front of the shopping centre. **Turn left at the end of the centre to walk past a couple of bus stops, heading for a red girder bridge. Before a set of traffic lights bear left on a path that leads through the subway under Redriff Road,** to emerge into fresh, unfamiliar surroundings.

Before you now is the ocean-liner sized expanse of Greenland Dock, tranquil now, but crowded with commercial shipping half a century ago. In operation by 1700, Howland Great Wet Dock, as it was first called, was surrounded by marshy, open land that would later be developed into the Surrey Commercial Docks.

These docks eventually extended to 370 acres, including a water area of 170 acres. A part of this busy scene was the Grand Surrey Canal, which by 1810 snaked over 3 miles from Rotherhithe to Camberwell, and later to Peckham.

Apart from general cargoes Greenland Dock, as its name suggests, was initially given over to the whaling industry, while timber and grain predominated in the rapidly expanding network of docks and 'ponds', where timber was stored, floating. This expansion revealed a slice of ancient history when in 1875, during excavations for a new tidal basin, a forest bed was discovered six feet down, which included some bones of a great ox.

Right: Mooring post on the dock edge, Russia Dock Woodland

Allied to Rotherhithe's already well-established and important ship-building, repairing, and breaking industries the Surrey Docks prospered well into the

20th century; some locals even have vivid memories of the outlandish sight of a 14,000 ton Cunard liner, on a regular visit to Greenland Dock, looming over the rooftops. Great damage was caused by wartime bombing, followed by major reconstruction, but after a flush of renewed success Surrey Docks' limited facilities just could not cope with the bigger ships of the day, leading to their rapid demise and closure in 1970.

Keep right to follow Thames Path signs, past a capstan and mooring post, and then go left along the far quayside. At the Watersports Centre, **turn right away from the water, then left after a dinghy storage area.** Carry on along Rope Street until South Dock appears on your right, with an interesting jumble of boats on display. **Cross a bridge and turn left into Rainbow Quay, and then go right to follow the water's edge again. Turn left to pass over the dock entrance,** with a grey arched footbridge adjacent.

If you fancy a break, try the 'Wibbley Wobbley' floating pub, a jaunty sight next to the quay, with its cosy, unsophisticated interior. You may see 'Sammy' moored near the bridge, a chunky, tough-looking U.S. Army tugboat, now somebody's home on the water. From the nearby riverside, the aspect of the giant office towers of Canary Wharf and the Isle of Dogs is quite dramatic, almost intimidating.

Turn left, now on the other side of the dock. Cross over Norway Cut Swing Bridge to walk along the water's edge to the inlet at the end of Finland Quay, with the Moby Dick pub just round this corner. **Leave the quayside to take a wide path ahead through a barrier under Redriff Road,** between grassy banks, following signs for Russia Dock Woodland. You can see some evidence of long-removed gates, and water height gauges, as this was the dock entrance. Shortly you **bear left to follow the granite edge and sturdy mooring-posts and chains of the filled-in dock.**

Set into this dockside path is a compass, engraved with evocative details of the array of goods that arrived here; 'Cape Farewell, Greenland. 1778 Miles. Whale Products'; 'Montreal, Canada. 3135 Miles. Wheat Dairy Produce.' Then a really distant destination: 'Calcutta India via Suez. 7965 Miles. Tea Jute Cotton Spices.' And so on.

Pass two bridges, and two barriers, then leave the dock edge to bear right, following the brick path, to arrive at a wooden bridge across an ornamental pond.

Here you have the opportunity to take an optional 1½ mile round trip to Nelson Dock, Lavender Pond Nature Park, and The Pumphouse Museum.

Optional Route...

Before the footbridge with its nautical iron 'Redriff' arch, **bear right to cross a side road to a brick path opposite, heading for brightly painted Redriff Primary School.** Continue, with the school's green wire fence on your left, to cross a footbridge over Salter Road. Keep ahead on Holyoake Footpath, **cross Rotherhithe Street and go straight ahead up a ramp to the riverside at Durand's Wharf.**

Looking across the water at so much high-rise wealth makes it very difficult to imagine the Isle of Dogs in Henry VIII's day, when it is said his kennels (hence the name) were located here on these low-lying marshlands to distance the king and his court, when in residence at Greenwich, from the baying of his hounds.

Turn left and continue for 300 yards, passing a barrier, until 25 yards before a small dock with a crane, you must **turn left, away from the river.** It's worth having a peep at the dock, where there is public access to the lock but no further, and then retracing your steps.

This is Nelson Dock, the best surviving fragment of Rotherhithe's shipbuilding past. Warships, merchantmen, and even steamships were built here and at other yards along this curve of riverbank, which from at least the 17th century was a very important maritime construction and repair centre. Nelson Dock was still in commercial use until 1968.

Right: La Dame de Serk at Nelson Dock

Walk away from the river past some low, garage-sized buildings then go right, skirting round the hotel buildings and the other end of Nelson Dock, heading for the mast of La Dame De Serk, which rests in a dry dock beside Nelson Dock House. Go down to the left of this old house **and turn right on Rotherhithe Street.** Continue past The Blacksmiths Arms and Canada Wharf, then **turn right up a concrete path** beside this restored warehouse to reach a flight of riverside stairs (to avoid steps here, continue along Rotherhithe Street to shortly arrive at a step-free access point).

These are Horns Stairs, old, worn, and slimy-green. At low tide you can see ancient timbers marking the line of a jetty, once used by a ferry to Limehouse.

From the stairs, continue upstream on the riverside pavement to pass a plain obelisk and then skirt around Pageant Stairs, with a view of Limehouse, and St Anne's Church, across the river. Cross a bridge over Lavender Dock entrance and then **turn left to leave the riverside and head for The Pumphouse Museum,** on the other side of Rotherhithe Street.

The Rotherhithe Heritage Museum is housed in the Pumphouse, which was originally used to maintain the water level in the docks. Now it is home to a fascinating display of local history, including clay pipes and other items found on the shore. There is also an illustrated description of the days when Peek Frean's biscuit factory provided thousands of local jobs, and the full story of the Surrey Commercial Docks, from the opening in 1700 of Howland Great Wet Dock, then through prosperous years when timber, grain, produce, and goods of every description were handled by a mostly casual labour force of dockers, to the final closure of the whole dock complex in 1970.Open Monday-Friday 09:00–17:00.

Keep to the right of Lavender Pond Nature Park, resplendent with reeds, alders, and waterfowl, and then **turn left on the pavement of Salter Road.** Walk 150 yards to Bywater Place and cross Salter Road. Leave the road here to **enter Russia Dock Woodland,** then keep to the high path and cross a footbridge. At a junction, **turn left over a footbridge** signed Stave Hill and Greenland Dock. This path curves around to arrive at a pond, where you go through a gate ahead signed Bacons College. Eventually you arrive at the other side of the footbridge graced with 'Redriff', where you turn right and rejoin the main route, following signs for Stave Hill.

The Main Route ...

Go over the wooden bridge, with its nautical iron 'Redriff' arch, and turn left, then right to Stave Hill. Pass through a barrier and then take either path round the hill to an ascending flight of steps.

The 'summit' of Stave Hill boasts a relief depiction of the former Surrey Commercial Docks' layout, and sweeping views to Canary Wharf, Crystal Palace, the London Eye, and Tower Bridge. Dominating the southerly aspect is the Evening Standard's printing works at Harmsworth Quays.

Go down the tree-lined slope of Dock Hill Avenue, with the City of London's 'Gherkin' dead ahead. Cross Timber Pond Road and Thame Road to pass a diminutive pagoda, whereupon you will emerge at Surrey Water, formerly Surrey Basin, a part of the old docks. **Turn left and follow the water's edge,** cross a lifting bridge, then turn left and continue along the right-hand side of this little watercourse, Albion Channel. Walk under a brick-arch bridge, and some way before a second bridge **turn right at a**

Right: Albion Channel, Surrey Water

cobbled ramp onto a path, Albatross Way, signed to Rotherhithe. Cross Needleman Street and then turn right when your path joins Swan Road. **Cross Albion Street,** then go over Brunel Road at the Adam and Eve pub and continue to a T-junction with Rotherhithe Street.

Just a few steps ahead here, by the statue of 'Sunshine Weekly and the Pilgrim's Pocket', is Cumberland Wharf. This pleasant spot affords a fine view, one of the best on the whole walk, of a great sweep of old riverside buildings; Gun Wharves, Metropolitan Wharf, and New Crane Wharf amongst others. To the right is the white-painted Prospect of Whitby pub on Wapping Wall. Behind this is the spire of St Mary's Cable Street, dating from 1850, and a little to the left is the older, more delicate St Paul's, Shadwell.

Turn left into Rotherhithe Street. Shortly on the left you will come across The Brunel Museum.

Motorists may be familiar with the nearby Rotherhithe Tunnel, which was completed in 1908, but Brunel's tunnel here was opened over sixty years beforehand. Father and son team Sir Marc and Isambard Kingdom Brunel completed this task, the world's first underwater tunnel, in 1843. During the 18 years of on-off construction several miners lost their lives, in fact the younger Brunel was lucky to survive a stroke, heart attack, and near-drowning. Flooding occurred more than once, and large quantities of clay had to be dumped from above to seal holes in the roof. It really was completed against all the odds. Designed to incorporate a spiral access ramp for wheeled traffic (which was never built), this pedestrian only twin-bore toll tunnel became a major tourist destination, attracting thousands of curious fee-paying visitors.

Sadly the tunnel's promoters, short of money, sold out to the East London Railway Company, which ran trains through from 1869 (these will soon be running

Right: St Mary's Church, Rotherhithe

Right: The Brunel
Museum tells the
story of the first
Thames tunnel

again on the rebuilt East London line). You can see
the tunnel portals from Rotherhithe and Wapping's
station platforms. The Brunel Museum has a wealth
of material relating to the tunnel's construction, and is
normally open 7 days 10:00-17:00.

**Continue ahead, and at the Mayflower pub
turn left,** into St Marychurch Street, then right, to
the front of the church.

This charming, unexpected, historic backwater is
Rotherhithe Village, a survivor of wartime bombs and
post-war town planners. At its centre is 18th-century St
Mary's Church, small but stylish. Huddled around the
church are the Mayflower pub, the Rotherhithe Picture
Library (housed in a solid old warehouse), and the Free
School of 1797. Standing guard over the graveyard, to
deter body-snatchers, is the Watch House.

Among the sea-captains and mariners buried here is
Lee Boo, a Prince on the Pacific island of Pelew, who
was brought to England by Captain Henry Wilson, who
had been shipwrecked on the island, in 1784. Sadly the
Prince succumbed to smallpox after only six months
of living and studying in Rotherhithe. His memorial,
behind some bushes near the church door, has this

inscription: 'Prince Lee Boo a native of the Pelew or Palos island and son to Abbe Thulle, Rupack or King of the island Coo'Roo'Raa. Died 27.12.84 age 20'.

Right: Clocktower of the former St Olave's School

Follow St Marychurch Street to the left, then at the Ship pub, turn right to follow Elephant Lane, which soon bears left to a riverside access point, signed 'Cherry Garden'. Continue through a covered way upstream towards Tower Bridge, passing the Angel inn, and a lifelike work of art depicting Dr Salter (who served the area for many years as a GP, and then as Member of Parliament for Bermondsey),his daughter, and her cat.

One lonely survivor of a workaday, tumbledown terrace of historic Thames-side buildings where Sir John Betjeman once lived, number 1 Fulford Street sits directly on the riverbank, as does its near neighbour, the Angel inn. King's Stairs (next to number 1) and Rotherhithe Stairs (next to the inn) are a reminder of bygone days when access to the river for watermen and their passengers was via these simple stairs, several of which are still in existence.

A map of 1872 shows several large granaries here, and a flour mill with its own millpond. Adjacent to Chambers Wharf stood a street-long rope works. Now you can only see the Millpond housing estate, and some unexpected remains of Edward III's moated manor house, strangely out of place here. A little further on, by the Old Justice pub, is the Duffield Sluice, part of a sewer scheme of 1822.

After skirting round Cherry Garden Pier, (a mooring point for Thames riverboat operators) and walking under some willow trees, **leave the riverside at Fountain Green Square** (by the drinking fountain) to **turn right, then left into Loftie Street. At its end turn right** and go past the former site of Chamber's Wharf. **Turn right into East Lane, then left to follow Bermondsey**

Wall West through a deep canyon of buildings. At Mill Street (divert a few yards left to a plaque which tells you what this area, at one time called Jacob's Island, used to be like), **continue up a narrow ramp with handrail,** signed to St Saviour's Dock. Go through a doorway to cross the dock entrance on a steel swing bridge.

Cast your eye down this most atmospheric and cavernous dock and recapture days of old; here were working wharves, granaries, a rice mill, and even a biscuit factory. The stream that flowed to this river outlet was called the Neckinger, perhaps because its meanders resembled a hangman's noose, and although now one of London's lost streams (there is barely a trickle at the dockhead) its name is still remembered in two local streets and a housing estate.

Follow the wide riverbank to the Design Museum (Maguire Street), here turn left then first right into Shad Thames. Continue ahead, past Curlew Street, then under Butler's Wharf's overhead walkways. **Take the next left** to follow Lafone Street, crossing two roads, to **arrive at a T-junction with Tooley Street. Turn right here.**

In this last three-quarters of a mile there is an exuberant display of architectural styles, including the tenements opposite (Devon Mansions of 1875, built before Tower Bridge existed), High Victorian grandeur (the former St Olave's Grammar School, 1893, next to Potter's Fields), and the stout, functional offices of the South Eastern Railway. Not to mention Hay's Wharf, Art Deco at St Olaf House, and new office blocks, like windswept glass monsters, at More London Place. You may prefer the homely attractions of the Shipwright's Arms, which sports a suitably nautical interior.

Follow Tooley Street, crossing Tower Bridge Road. Continue on for a further 1/3 mile to London Bridge station and walk's end.

The North-West Frontier

Holland Park to Hendon in four stages

Infinite contrasts and unexpected pleasures of waterside and parkland walking are the rewards for the intrepid voyager to the North-West Frontier. Award-winning parks, workaday streets, a peaceful canalside, and the wooded banks of a reservoir lead to a 17th-century farmhouse, with church and pub next door, near the edge of what could almost be open country.

Stage One: Holland Park to Harlesden (Willesden Junction)

Distance 3½ miles. Intermediate distances: Kensington Leisure Centre 1 mile, Wormwood Scrubs 2 miles, Old Oak Lane 3 miles.

Time 2 hours.

Terrain Virtually all paved, with some modest gradients. There are steps down to the canal towpath.

Refreshments Cafés and a pub at Holland Park Avenue, pubs in Princedale Road, cafés at Clarendon Cross and Kensington Leisure Centre, also some choice in Latimer Road, North Pole Road and Old Oak Lane.

Toilets Avondale Park, Kensington Leisure Centre, Willesden Junction station.

Transport Fare zones 2 & 3. Holland Park (Tube, bus), Latimer Road (Tube, bus), Willesden Junction (Tube, train, bus).

Best time to do the walk At any time, any day of the week.

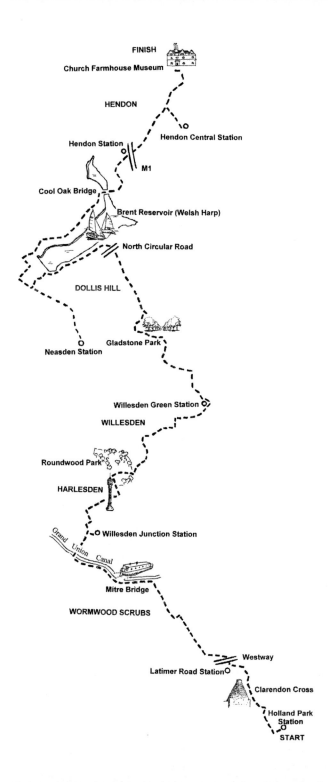

FINISH

Church Farmhouse Museum

HENDON

Hendon Central Station

Hendon Station

M1

Cool Oak Bridge

Brent Reservoir (Welsh Harp)

North Circular Road

DOLLIS HILL

Gladstone Park

Neasden Station

Willesden Green Station

WILLESDEN

Roundwood Park

HARLESDEN

Willesden Junction Station

Grand Union Canal

Mitre Bridge

WORMWOOD SCRUBS

Westway

Latimer Road Station

Clarendon Cross

Holland Park Station

START

There are plenty of places to part with your money clustered around Holland Park station, including a tempting patisserie, a well-stocked bookshop, Lidgate, the traditional butcher, offering seasonal produce such as 'fresh grouse from Yorkshire', and the tile-fronted Castle pub.

Start at Holland Park station (Central line). Turn right out of the station to **follow Holland Park Avenue**, crossing first Clarendon Road and then Portland Road. Take the **next right to follow Princedale Road,** with Norland Place, a well-kept mews on the left, worthy of an admiring glance. Pass the Prince of Wales pub, and, on the left, Penzance Street, and then turn right into Penzance Place. Cross Pottery Lane and keep on ahead to **join Portland Road at Clarendon Cross.**

Left: Clarendon Cross provides some shade on a hot day

It's tempting to take a break on one of the benches in this pleasant backwater, but the walk has only just started. Anyway, Avondale Park is only round the corner.

Take the first left into Hippodrome Place, then turn right to follow Walmer Road.

Quite suddenly you arrive in the area previously known as the Potteries, borne out by the surprising sight of a

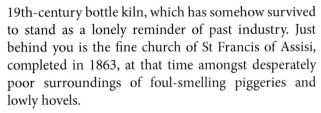

19th-century bottle kiln, which has somehow survived to stand as a lonely reminder of past industry. Just behind you is the fine church of St Francis of Assisi, completed in 1863, at that time amongst desperately poor surroundings of foul-smelling piggeries and lowly hovels.

Above: A surprising relic of past industry in 'The Potteries'

Below: Avondale Park displays fine floral beds, and a small wilderness garden

Hippodrome Place recalls the short-lived racecourse of the same name, an over-ambitious project covering nearly 200 acres with an entrance at Notting Hill Gate. It was deeply unpopular, both with the locals because it severed a much-used footpath, and with the jockeys who had to contend with heavy going on the clay soil. This huge white elephant of a scheme fizzled out within five years, closing in 1842.

Opposite the kiln, **enter Avondale Park through a gate,** then go straight ahead between two small buildings (there are toilets in the left-hand building), and then **turn right alongside tennis courts,** passing a tiny wildlife garden. Carry on ahead to **leave the park, then do a quick right and left to follow Avondale Park Road,** aiming for the neat little spire of Notting Hill Methodist Church.

At the end of this road **turn right, then go left to pass the Kensington Leisure Centre** (there are toilets and a café here). Now the road bends to the right, and on the bend you **turn left into Verity Close.** Head for a barrier on the right, at the end of Verity Close, then go through another barrier and **turn left to arrive in Lancaster Road**, facing the Methodist Church. **Turn left and continue round a right-hand bend to follow Silchester Road.** Press on under a railway bridge and at the end of the road

turn right to follow Bramley Road (a left turn will bring you to Latimer Road station).

In 1970, the A40 Westway opened to traffic. Although it eased the motorist's lot, the disruption, displacement, and destruction suffered by the local population was severe and immediate. One group of spirited residents, incensed by officialdom's callous re-zoning of their now-dilapidated neighbourhood for industrial units, set up their own mini-state in 1977; the Free Independent Republic of Frestonia, based in Freston Road, which is just past Latimer Road station. Consisting of a land area of one acre, and with 120 inhabitants, this marvel of modern democracy nevertheless managed, by dint of a great deal of campaigning, publicity, and even an appeal to the United Nations, to ensure that common sense, and even their own housing plans, won the day.

Left: Climbing practice under the Westway

Immediately after going under the Westway bridge, **turn left into Crowthorne Road,** then follow a walkway ahead between the Westway Sports Centre's pitches, parallel with the curving concrete highway high above you.

Occupying this strange sun-starved world under west London's own spaghetti junction are some surprising sights: another little wildlife garden, the sports centre's frighteningly overhanging climbing wall, and the Westway Stables horse exercise ring.

Bear right, past the sports centre buildings, then a little to the left, to eventually leave the Westway's shadow at the horse exercise ring and turn right to follow Latimer Road.

Latimer Road certainly has variety. Attractive old brick-built studio workshops sit side-by-side with the Tabernacle Christian Centre, while a terrace of comfortable-looking cottages faces a row of small factory units. On the corner of Snarsgate Street the Thai River Café is almost completely shrouded in ivy and mature vines, then at the top of the road the North Pole pub, and to the left, at the junction with Wood Lane, The Pavilion, offer sustenance to give you strength for the last couple of miles of the walk.

At North Pole Road, cross over to carry on ahead along Bracewell Road. This road ends at Dalgarno Gardens, with Little Wormwood Scrubs open space opposite. **Turn left into Mitre Way, go under the bridge, then turn right for a few yards to cross Scrubs Lane** at the zebra crossing. Go through a hedge gap to **turn right on a brick path** which you follow through the wooded edge of Wormwood Scrubs Park. Alternatively, you can keep on ahead to stay clear of the trees, and follow a parallel route on the open grass to join up with the brick path later on, at an obvious clearing.

Across the wide-open grassland are the Linford Christie Stadium, Hammersmith Hospital, and glimpses of Wormwood Scrubs Prison. Several parts of 'The Scrubs' are designated Local Nature Reserves, occasionally disturbed by troops from the Royal Horse Artillery who practise here for the Royal Tournament.

Eventually **the brick path leads back to Scrubs Lane, where your route turns left** to continue under a bridge, going gently uphill. Now the railways begin to encroach on every side, with both road and rail making use of rusty lattice-girder iron bridges. **Once across the railway, at Mitre Bridge, go down a flight of steps on the left to join the canal towpath,** and carry on ahead with trains to your left and a few houseboats on the right.

You are now on the Paddington Arm of the Grand Union Canal, 13½ miles of lock-free tranquillity. This waterway provides access from London's docks and wharves, via the Regent's Canal, to the Grand Union Canal main line at Bull's Bridge, Southall. It is quite possible to walk, or cycle, from Paddington, or even Limehouse, as far as you like towards Birmingham; but the towpath is not always as easy as this ¾ mile stretch that you now follow.

Left: On the Grand Union Canal near Mitre Bridge

Opened in 1801 after taking six years to construct, the canal very soon faced intense competition from the burgeoning rail network, and a quick peep over the wall, or a glance to the left where the wall ends, provides the answer to the winner of that contest, with acres of gleaming rails and speeding Great Western trains, plus the North Pole International train depot, all looking very busy.

Press on along the towpath, passing an area of birch woodland. Away to the left are sidings crammed with elderly rolling stock. Ancient diesel engines slumber peacefully in serried ranks. Carry on past the gigantic Powerday recycling plant, where a new wharf has been constructed for a planned return to canal transport of bulk materials. Just after this, **go under a low railway bridge and immediately left up a ramp to Old Oak Lane.**

Until the amalgamation of a group of canals in 1929 the waterway you have just walked alongside went by the name of the Grand Junction Canal, and you may notice a boundary marker on the ramp here; 'G J C Co'.

Turn right on Old Oak Lane, back over the canal, and keep going past The Fisherman's Arms and a hamlet of ex-railwaymen's cottages, reminiscent more of a Midlands railway town than a London suburb. Even the street names evoke railway history: Crewe Place, Stephenson Street, and Stoke Place. Keep on ahead, over more railway lines, to Willesden Junction station (there are toilets on the platforms) and the end of Stage One.

Right: This section of the walk is steeped in railway history

Stage Two: Harlesden (Willesden Junction) to Willesden Green

Distance 2¼ miles. Intermediate distance: Roundwood Park 1 mile.

Time 1½ hours.

Terrain Mostly level paving or tarmac paths.

Refreshments Some choice in Harlesden, the Park Café in Roundwood Park, and a few cafés, pubs, and takeaways in Willesden Green.

Toilets On platforms 1 and 3 at Willesden Junction station, Harlesden Plaza, Roundwood Park, Willesden Green Library.

Transport Fare zones 2 & 3. Willesden Junction (Tube, train, bus), Willesden Green (Tube, bus).

Best time to do the walk Anytime, but perhaps best from April onwards, when the floral beds in Roundwood Park are superb.

Right: Harlesden's
well-kept
Jubilee clock

Willesden Junction station is a bit confusing. In fact, it is said that the ghost of a passenger, hopelessly lost, still wanders the walkways and footbridges looking for the exit from 'Bewildering Junction' as it was known. Not all the routes from here were an instant success; the line to Clapham Junction originally ended at Kensington, and was known as 'Mr Punch's railway', a rather comical enterprise with no proper terminus. The inaugural run carried just one passenger, a lone winkle-seller.

Start at Willesden Junction station (trains from Euston-Watford Junction, Clapham Junction, North London line, and Bakerloo line). **Take the exit for Old Oak Lane,** into which you turn right. **Cross Tubbs Road and take the next right into Honeywood Road,** with the Willesden Junction Hotel on the corner. **Go to the very end of this side street,** passing Ranelagh Road, and then **turn left up a part-cobbled back way, Avenue Road.** At the end of this road, with All Souls church to your left, **turn right to follow Station Road.** Cross left to the island on which stands Harlesden's Jubilee Clock.

This elegant timepiece of 1887, the 50th year of Queen Victoria's reign, featured in a photograph taken in 1908 depicting 'Dorando, Italy, First in the Stadium'. Harlesden was on the route of the London Olympics Marathon of that year, Dorando was in the lead, but as he neared the finishing line at White City Stadium exhaustion overcame him, he stumbled and was helped by a spectator, and with that help came disqualification. Although he lost the gold medal, he won the hearts of the crowd, including Queen Alexandra who presented him with a gold cup the following day.

In common with most of suburban London, Harlesden only developed with the arrival of railways in the latter part of the 19th century, the success of which can be judged by some of the attractions offered around 1900 by the London and North-Western Railway at Willesden Junction, with 'Frequent trains to Euston, Broad Street, Mansion House, Victoria ... Royal Mail route to Birmingham, Liverpool ... Sleeping Saloons, Dining and Drawing Room Cars.' A glance at this area on a London street map shows the continuing importance of the local rail connections.

For centuries before this rapid expansion Harlesden was agricultural, just a hamlet of less than 100 souls at the time of the Domesday Book survey of 1086. Nowadays the town is bustling with a rich mix of cultures, but apart from new shop fronts, and the international choice of goods on offer, this unpretentious Victorian suburb still retains a pleasingly undeveloped atmosphere.

From the clock, cross right to continue in the same direction, now on Harlesden High Street's left-hand pavement (or turn left on the High Street for toilets, 100 yards along, in The Plaza). Cross Manor Park Road (with the Royal Oak pub to your right) and **keep going along Park Parade,** glancing across the road to see 'The Workers' on the corner of Rucklidge Avenue, all three of them, sculpted in iron for the 'Art in the City' project. Continue past the shops to a roundabout. **Turn left into Harlesden Road, then left again to follow Longstone Avenue.** Keep going past a large expanse of grass on the right, then at a roundabout junction with Drayton Park carry on for a few yards to **cross right at a zebra crossing and go through a gate into Roundwood Park.**

Opened in 1895, Roundwood Park could show some public parks in wealthier parts of the capital a thing or two. The Surveyor to the Local Board, O C Robson, laid out the park, and was enthusiastically credited with having created 'a veritable Garden of Eden without the serpents' by the Chairman of the Parks Committee at the opening ceremony. Curving paths lead to a breezy

Above: Roundwood Park offers beautiful floral displays, a good café, and plenty of benches to relax on

hilltop area, at one time graced with a bandstand, then meander back down to the Park Café, the sort of child-friendly, good-value establishment that every park needs. Near the imposing wrought-iron main gates is the fine lodge-house, built for the lucky gardener, and an elaborate, weathervane-topped drinking fountain. Away to the left is the Summer Theatre, built in 1959, which used to be a popular venue for children's open-air shows, but is no longer used. The real attention-grabber, though, is the flower-filled corner of the park, alive with luscious blooms in neat beds of glorious colour, by its appearance a labour of love for the council's gardeners. The park has earned an astonishing nine consecutive Civic Trust Green Flag awards up to 2007/8, for its high standards throughout.

Until being demolished in 1937 a grand Victorian mansion stood nearby. This was Roundwood House, home to George Furness and his family. A man of many talents, he was first and foremost a civil engineering contractor, who took on projects as far afield as Russia and Brazil, which was no mean feat in the mid 1800s. He also played a major part in Willesden's local affairs and development, even running his own brickworks in Chambers Lane. In London, he worked with Sir Joseph Bazalgette on the construction of the Thames Embankments. As you continue your walk, you will pass some of the cottages he had built for his workers to rent, in Parkfield Road. He was, perhaps, Willesden's foremost resident.

For a glimpse of the Wembley Arch follow the path to the top of the hill, otherwise keep on ahead past the Park Café (there are toilets in the café, and further on, to the left of the drinking fountain). **Leave the park through the ornate main gates** and go half-right across the roadway and a paved path between weeping willow trees to **cross Harlesden Road at a zebra crossing.** Turn left and follow this road as it swings right at a roundabout and continues gently uphill, crossing Donnington Road, to arrive at another roundabout and junction. Just stay on the right-hand pavement to follow the winding course of Harlesden Road, whose kinks and curves, reminiscent of a country lane, snaked their way to the old village of Willesden Green long before the surrounding streets were built. Pass Parkfield Road, which is lined with Victorian cottages, then St Mary Magdalen's Catholic Church, and the Rising Sun pub. Take the next left to **follow Grange Road, with Willesden Green Library Centre on the right,** where you will find a café, toilets, and the Brent Museum.

Next to the library is the Willesden Bookshop, with plenty of titles featuring London, and local, history on sale amongst their large stock. Fronting the main road is a decorative portion of the original library of 1894 that was spared demolition in the 1980s, when the new building appeared.

Several local roads, built when the Metropolitan Railway from Baker Street to Harrow opened up this area to development from 1880 onwards, are reminders of the previous landowners hereabouts; the Dean and Chapter of St Paul's Cathedral. Hence Dean Road, Chapter Road, and St Paul's Avenue (which was at first part of Chapter Road, but was renamed after complaints of the poorer western end of the road lowering the tone).

Grange Road meets Willesden High Road, which you cross, and then turn right. Continue past parades of shops, crossing Park Avenue, to eventually come to a junction and traffic lights. Swing left along Walm Lane to shortly arrive at Willesden Green station (Jubilee line), and the end of Stage Two of your walk.

Stage Three: Willesden Green to Neasden

Distance 3 miles. Intermediate distances: Dollis Hill 1 mile, Brook Road footbridge 2 miles.

Time 1½ -2 hours.

Terrain Pavement, tarmac paths with some moderate gradients, one footbridge with a ramp, gravel paths and grassed areas around the reservoir.

Refreshments Willesden Green, Gladstone Park (Thursday-Sunday), Neasden.

Toilets Willesden Green, Gladstone Park.

Transport Fare zones 2 & 3. Willesden Green (Tube, bus), Dollis Hill (½ mile off route), (Tube, bus), Neasden Lane North (buses to Neasden station, Jubilee line).

Best time to do the walk
As with Stage Two, go when the floral beds, this time in Gladstone Park, are at their best.

Above and right:
There are several pleasant surprises in Gladstone Park, including these tree sculptures, and an award-winning walled garden

Sometimes place names are a reminder of a well-known local farm, building, or landowner, and this may be the case with Dollis Hill, which merited inclusion in some old maps as 'Dolley's Hill'; perhaps named after a farmer or person of note who lived here.

Start at Willesden Green station (Jubilee line). **Turn left out of the station, then immediately left to follow Station Parade.** At a right-hand bend, by an individual house, 'The Castle', **turn left to follow Riffel Road. Keep going along this road as it bears right and eventually comes to a T-junction with Melrose Avenue. Turn left** and follow this pleasant residential backwater to a roundabout junction with Anson Road, with Gladstone Park opposite. Turn left, cross at the refuge, then go a few yards left to **enter the park.**

Right: This ornamental pond graces the hilltop in Gladstone Park

This welcome expanse of rural bliss amongst the suburbs was named after William Gladstone, several times Prime Minister in the late 1800s. He liked to escape from Westminster to the tranquillity of Dollis Hill House, home of Lord and Lady Aberdeen, whose house and grounds formed the nucleus of the park when it was created. Gladstone Park, which opened in 1901, came into being when the local council managed to buy the surrounding land to stem the relentless advance of bricks and mortar. Again, this park has won several Green Flag awards in recent years.

Keep ahead on the tarmac path, which soon rises to cross a railway line.

From the bridge, there are points of interest for the railway enthusiast; a working signalbox at 'Dudding Hill Junction', and to the west, semaphore signals. This line was not one of the winners in the late 19th-century rivalry for passengers; in fact it was built mainly for goods traffic, and now usually carries only freight trains. Providing a link between Hendon and

Acton, the line came into being in 1868, operated by the Midland and South Western Junction Railway.

Once over the railway bridge, take the main, left-hand path, which is canopied with London plane trees. Some interesting wood-carvings enliven the scene here. At a crossing track by a children's playground, keep straight ahead, uphill (Dollis Hill station, on the Jubilee line, can be reached by turning left here).

Turn right at the next junction to enter a fenced area, then turn right alongside a duck pond, standing in which is an elegant statue. Keep on ahead to go through an arched opening in a brick wall to enter a flower-filled walled garden. The Karmarama café, with tables grouped around a secluded courtyard, is through a gate on the left, where there is also a toilet.

This was the kitchen garden of Dollis Hill House, where Gladstone enjoyed helping himself to fresh strawberries in season during his pre-breakfast walks, and was rejuvenated as an 'Old English Garden' a few years after Gladstone Park opened to the public. The freshness and colour of the beds and borders are quite exceptional, and fittingly this garden won the London in Bloom Best Bedding Display award in 2005. If you have time, take advantage of the chance to rest awhile in this fragrant little hideaway. The old house, built in 1825, stands next door, awaiting major restoration or demolition if no economic use can be found for it.

Left: Dudding Hill Junction, with working signal box and semaphore signals

Turn right to leave the garden, then left to leave the park opposite Neville's Court. Turn left, cross Dollis Hill Lane, then turn right to follow Brook Road.

At the crest of the hill, opposite a covered reservoir, is Chartwell Court, now private dwellings, but formerly the Post Office Research station. With its green copper dome, it dominates this airy hilltop site looking out over the Brent Valley. Underneath this building, 40 ft below ground and encased in bomb-proof concrete, is a secret World War Two command bunker, codenamed 'Paddock'.

If Westminster became too dangerous for the War Cabinet to operate, the plan was to decamp here, and for several years the bunker was staffed and ready for use. Meetings of top brass were held in the depths of this citadel, one of which Winston Churchill attended. Eventually a more central location was chosen and the bunker was locked up and abandoned in 1944. Over a period of nearly sixty years the underground rooms, sealed and forgotten, became damp and dilapidated, but with the recent housing development of the above-ground buildings, the bunker has been re-opened for guided tours twice a year, including over the Open House weekend in September.

Continue downhill on Brook Road, crossing Crest Road at a roundabout. At the end of Brook Road a footbridge provides your passport to the other side of the North Circular Road, where you **step through a gate to follow a cinder track** snaking its way through Neasden Recreation Ground. As this path progresses, you can divert to a parallel waterside route through lush greenery, with glimpses of the open waters of the Brent Reservoir. This way rejoins the cinder track later on.

The Brent Reservoir, or Welsh Harp, was constructed 1835–37 to satisfy the increasingly thirsty Grand Union Canal, and to augment existing supplies from Aldenham, Ruislip, and the still-functioning canal feeder, which since 1811 has tapped the River Brent. The feeder flows 3¼ miles to the canal at Lower Place, near Harlesden station. Later on, your walk crosses both this modest little waterway and the river.

Many years ago, near the eastern end of the reservoir, on the Edgware Road, stood a popular inn called the

Welsh Harp. In its heyday the inn drew crowds from far and wide who came to sample the music hall, or refresh themselves after a visit to the nearby racecourse. There was also a zoo, from which a bear once escaped and, heading for Hendon, caused more than a little panic amongst the locals before being recaptured. The inn has long gone; swept away in 1971 to make room for the Staples Corner flyover, but the name lives on.

At an information point, follow the right-hand edge of a grassed area alongside a wire fence, passing the inaccessible face of the dam. When you come to the end of the wire fence keep on ahead for 100 yards on a faint track to **locate a ramp on your right leading down to an exit between houses, emerging onto Braemar Avenue.**

Gravel Pit Farm, one of Neasden's last vestiges of countryside, used to be here. Apart from gravel digging, the farm had cattle, pigs, and in 1907, the last registered sheepdog in the area. In 1928 the farm was sold after suffering an outbreak of foot-and-mouth disease the year before, and by 1936 these houses had been built.

Turn left and continue to a junction, where you turn left again, still on Braemar Avenue. At the end of this road **turn right into Neasden Lane North,** where Stage Three of your walk ends. There are regular buses from here to Neasden station on the Jubilee line (Route 297, journey time 5–10 minutes) which stop at Neasden Parade, which offers one or two cafés and pubs. If you prefer to walk, the station is 20 minutes away via brightly tiled Neasden Subway and a footbridge over the underpass.

Stage Four: Neasden to Hendon

Distance 3¾ miles.
Intermediate distances: Welsh
Harp Open Space 1 mile,
Hendon (Station Road) 2 miles,
Church End, Hendon 3 miles.

Time 2–2½ hours.

Terrain Mostly paved, with a
gentle uphill stretch to Hendon.
There is an undulating gravel
track beside the Brent Reservoir.

Refreshments Neasden Parade
(1/3 mile off route), Greenhouse
Garden Centre café, and a choice
of pubs and cafés in Hendon.

Toilets Greenhouse Garden
Centre, Hendon Library.

Transport Fare zones 3 & 4.
Neasden Lane North (buses
to Neasden station, Jubilee
line), Hendon (train, bus),
Hendon Central (Tube, bus).

Best time to do the walk
Pick a warm day so you can
picnic beside the Welsh Harp,
or make an autumn visit to spot
migrating water-loving birds.

Right: Making the
most of a breeze on
the Welsh Harp

For years Neasden has been the butt of many a comedian's jokes, portrayed as the sort of faceless suburb that nobody wants to end up in. Before the days of rail travel, the little hamlet of Neasden, up on the hill to your left (Neasden Parade is still there, clinging on to life while the North Circular traffic howls past), was surrounded by farmland, a golf course, the well-known firm of Tattersalls' stud farm, and even a rest home for horses. Citizens of influence resided here; included in the census of 1851 were a mere 95 inhabitants, but amongst these were a stockbroker, three lawyers at Lincoln's Inn, and a manager at the Royal Mint.

Looking across the careering lanes of traffic on Neasden Lane North provides a clue to the rapid change that came about here from the 1880s onwards; those tall, rather gloomy houses opposite Braemar Avenue are part of an estate built in the fields of Neasden Bottom in 1882 to house workers at the Metropolitan Railway's nearby depot, at a time when the fields and farms hereabouts were soon to be swallowed up by street upon street of suburbia as the railway relentlessly pushed further into open country.

Start opposite the Quainton Street Open Space, on Neasden Lane North, near the junction with Braemar Avenue. There are frequent buses from both Kingsbury and Neasden that stop at Quainton Street. **Follow Neasden Lane North,** crossing first the canal feeder, lazily flowing along its two-century old course, and then the River Brent, as it continues on its journey to join the Thames at Brentford. Now you are on Blackbird Hill. **Take the first right, Birchen Grove**. After 250 yards, at a footpath sign, **turn left to follow Church Walk.** At the end of this path **turn right to follow Old Church Lane**, which also bears the sign 'Old St Andrew's Mansions'.

Across the road, half-hidden in a thick copse of trees, is 'old' St Andrew's Church, Kingsbury, which became redundant in 1977. This ancient place of worship, which recent archaeological work has shown to date from the 11th century, is one of the oldest churches in Middlesex. It contains three rare bells, one dating from 1340 which is said to be the oldest hanging bell in the county. The walls incorporate some flint and bricks re-used from a Roman building, giving rise to the romantic legend that these were from a camp used by Julius Caesar's legions, who probably passed by here on their way to do battle with an unruly British tribe in Hertfordshire.

Above: 'Old' St Andrew's Church, Kingsbury

Beyond the old church you may get a glimpse of the stately outline of 'new' St Andrew's, built 1845–47 in Wells Street, near Oxford Circus and itself declared redundant in 1931. The whole building was then carefully dismantled and re-erected at this site by 1934.

Below: 'New' St Andrew's Church

Continue to the end of Old Church Lane, passing a pumping station, and turn left along Birchen Grove. Follow this road as it swings right (or go straight ahead for 300 yards to the Greenhouse Garden Centre, which has a café and toilets). Very soon the road peters out at the Welsh Harp Open Space car park. **Pass the car park entrance and bear right to follow a tarmac path with waterside views.**

Pause for a moment at the information point here to read about the history and wildlife of the reservoir, and to learn some rules for the sailing competitions that are a regular feature on the water.

Keep ahead on this path, which later becomes a gravel track. Pass the unpretentious home of the North Circular Sailing Club, then a sports field. Eventually the path twists and turns its way to **emerge at Cool Oak Bridge, which you must cross** with the aid of a push-button traffic light control.

To your left as you cross the bridge is the picturesque valley of the Silk Stream, providing a happy home for all sorts of water-loving birds, while unseen away to the right the River Brent adds its quota to the still waters. Together these watercourses and their tributaries drain a large area of north London's hills, from Highgate to Edgware and beyond.

You are now on Cool Oak Lane. **Carry on ahead to a T-junction with West Hendon Broadway.** Cross this busy thoroughfare with care at the lights and then **turn left. Walk past Park Road and Brent View Road, then take the next right to follow Station Road.** Continue past Hendon station (Thameslink trains to Blackfriars, King's Cross, and south London), and keep going for half a mile to the junction with A41 Watford Way. **Go through the subway to carry on in the same direction along The Burroughs, passing the White Bear pub.** Use the pedestrian crossing by the library (toilets and café here) to continue on the left-hand pavement.

For over 150 years Hendon Fair, held near the White Bear, entertained the locals with dancing and all manner of country pursuits, and served as a hiring fair where Irish workers would find jobs on Hendon's hay farms. Hay would be delivered to feed London's horses, with a return load of manure to spread on the fields. The fair survived until the late 1800s, and one last active farm, Church End, clung on until 1967.

As you progress along The Burroughs (there used to be rabbit warrens here), there are several buildings of note: the elaborate many-windowed Town Hall (built 1901), library (1929), and fire station (1914). Further on is the businesslike shape of Middlesex University, dating from the late 1930s.

Pass the University, follow the road as it bears right, then take the first left, Church

End. Daniel's Almshouses, which are opposite, were founded in 1729. They were rebuilt in 1800 and are still lived in. **Keep going past the Chequers pub, crossing with care to the right-hand pavement,** to arrive at a cluster of cherished old buildings: St Mary's Church, Church Farmhouse Museum, and the Greyhound pub.

Some of the fabric of St Mary's dates from the 13th century, making it Hendon's oldest building. The 50 ft tower was added around 1450, and then the church was extended eastwards 1913–15. Probably the best-known individual to be buried in the church is Sir Stamford Raffles (1781–1826), founder of London Zoo, and, in 1819, Singapore.

Young's real ales are available at the Greyhound, next door to the church. This cosy old inn dates from 1898 and is the third building on this site, the first one having burnt down in 1676. Nearly 200 years after this event, the need for some sort of fire protection led to the local Volunteer Fire Brigade stabling their engine opposite the church.

17th-century Church Farmhouse, strategically placed by church and pub to create the perfect village nucleus, rejoices in the title of Hendon's second oldest building. A wealth of local history and information is contained in the museum here, including the story of Hendon Aerodrome, from where in 1910 a Frenchman, Louis Paulhan, flew to Manchester in a little over four hours to win a £10,000 prize put up by the Daily Mail. Pageants staged by the RAF were a very popular annual event for many years, but there was no room for the airport to expand, and the site is now a housing estate. Memories still linger on, with the RAF Museum and the Metropolitan Police College occupying parts of the old airfield.

There is a garden behind Church Farmhouse Museum. **Walk to a gate at the end of the path** through

this peaceful little green space, from where the aspect is mostly rural; this is part of Sunny Hill Park, but it might as well be the hayfields of old Hendon. For a moment, savour this rustic and delightful spot, the turning point of The North-West Frontier walk, a place where the tantalizing feeling of open country almost within your grasp is enhanced by the verdant parkland slopes that fill the foreground, before returning to the pub and church.

It's been quite a journey, from the bustle of Holland Park to this suburban spot, but the variety of places

visited on the way, coupled with a little bit of historical background, may have helped the miles speed by. Take your pick of Hendon's pubs, or perhaps the café at Hendon Central station, to raise a celebratory glass and reflect on all those interesting corners of London that you've discovered. Well done.

From here it is just a matter of retracing your steps back past the White Bear to Watford Way, where a left turn will bring you, after ¼ mile, to Hendon Central station, for Northern line trains.

8 Peaks and Troughs

Wood Green to Notting Hill in four stages

Unrivalled views from Alexandra Palace, Parliament Hill, and Primrose Hill, embellished with Highgate Village's fascinating history and buildings, are the focus of this walk, which continues along the Regent's and Grand Union canals, then through the amazing variety of Portobello Road to the final 'peak' at Notting Hill.

Stage One: Wood Green to Highgate Village

Distance 4 miles. Intermediate distances: Alexandra Palace 1¼ miles, Muswell Hill 2 miles, Highgate Wood 3 miles.

Time 3 hours.

Terrain Some steep gradients, a few steps (which can be easily avoided), and a long stretch of woodland paths, which may be muddy.

Refreshments Wood Green has plenty of pubs and cafés. Alexandra Park has a café by the boating lake, the Phoenix bar at Palm Court, and the Grove café. There are plenty of places to eat, drink, and be merry in Muswell Hill, including the Crocodile Garden Café. The café at Highgate Wood is a treat, and Highgate Village has some good pubs, one or two baker's shops and cafés, and the popular Village Deli.

Toilets Wood Green, Alexandra Palace, Muswell Hill, Highgate Wood and Village.

Transport Fare zones 2 & 3. Wood Green (Tube, bus), Alexandra Palace (train, bus), Muswell Hill (bus), Highgate (Tube, bus), Highgate Village (bus), Archway (Tube, bus).

Best time to do the walk Pick a clear day to appreciate the far-reaching views.

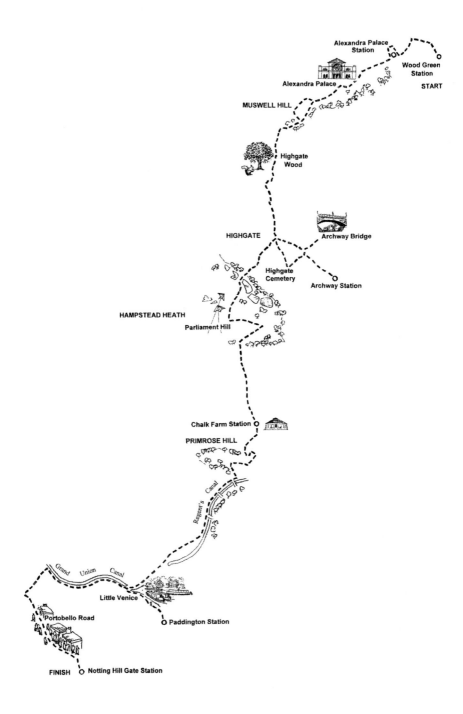

Alexandra Palace
Station

Wood Green
Station

START

Alexandra Palace

MUSWELL HILL

Highgate
Wood

HIGHGATE

Archway Bridge

Highgate
Cemetery

Archway Station

HAMPSTEAD HEATH

Parliament Hill

Chalk Farm Station

PRIMROSE HILL

Regent's Canal

Grand Union Canal

Little Venice

Portobello Road

Paddington Station

FINISH   Notting Hill Gate Station

E merging from Wood Green's Art Deco station concourse, a rooftop sign away to your left announces the presence of Shopping City, a huge, no-nonsense shopper's paradise, opened by The Queen on 13 May 1981. Your route, however, steers well clear of this retail Mecca to see some older parts of the town.

Start from Wood Green station (Piccadilly line). Cross High Road at the traffic lights (turn left for toilets at the library, 250 yards down on the right, or at Shopping City), and **turn right, uphill,** towards the prominent spire of St Michael's Church, passing the cavernous bus depot on the way. At the church, **turn left to follow Bounds Green Road,** passing several rose-bedecked cottages.

These humble dwellings date from the early 1800s, and are some of the oldest houses in Wood Green. Across the road the grassy, tree-shaded triangle is Trinity Gardens, behind which is the Greek Orthodox Cathedral of St Mary (originally a Methodist chapel of 1871), and a little further on, an obelisk complete with drinking fountains commemorating Mrs Catharine Smithies, a local temperance campaigner, placed uncomfortably close to the 'Prince' pub, which exhibits in the doorway a tiled display of the Prince of Wales' feathers.

At the traffic lights turn left into Park Avenue, which you follow to a T-junction with Station Road. Just before Station Road you will cross the New River (note the New River Path signs here), which despite its name has been supplying north London with fresh Hertfordshire water for nearly 400 years.

This remarkable man-made channel, originally 38 miles in length, was completed in 1613 by Sir Hugh Myddelton, a very determined man, who eventually had to enlist the financial and moral support of the

King (James I) to complete the work. The river follows the 100 ft contour, with a fall of only 18 ft from the source to the old terminus at New River Head, Sadler's Wells, from where supplies were piped to the City. Although the river now ends at Stoke Newington, it is still a vital part of London's water supply. It can be seen issuing from a tunnel to your left here.

Turn right at Station Road (or cut the corner using the path across Avenue Gardens) to Alexandra Palace station. **Cross at the pedestrian lights to follow a footpath to the right of the station buildings,** taking you high above the platforms. Soon you will **emerge on Bedford Road, which you cross** with care, using the refuge 25 yards to the right if necessary. **Turn left to follow the pavement, which enters Alexandra Park** and soon becomes a rising path through a parade of chestnut trees. At a crossing track, turn right then first left, going uphill again, and continuing through the Rose Garden with the grand bulk of Alexandra Palace dead ahead, and the Ice Rink entrance in view. **Bear left across the car park, towards the transmission tower, to follow the terrace along the front of the building,** from where the view extends on a clear day to the hilltop mast at Crystal Palace, south London's high spot, and the chimneys and towers of the Thames Estuary.

Alexandra Palace, named after Princess Alexandra, Princess of Wales, opened in 1873 as a north London rival to Crystal Palace, which had opened its doors to the public a few years previously. It was instantly popular, with a bank holiday attendance shortly after it opened of 60,000, but these good times were not to last. Only sixteen days after the grand opening a fire broke out on the roof, caused by a workman's charcoal brazier, and within 1½ hours the building was a sad ruin.

Left: Alexandra Palace sits in a commanding hilltop position, and enjoys far-reaching views

Victorian entrepreneurs did not give up easily, and two years later a new palace rose out of the ashes. Housed in the Great Hall was the huge Willis Organ, worked by giant bellows which were driven by two steam engines. Also on display were an Italian garden, Egyptian, Japanese, and Moorish villages, and a circus. This was all very impressive, but before long fashions changed, the public tired of these displays, and the palace went into a slow decline.

Later, in the 1914–18 War, it was used to house refugees, then it became an internment camp. There was a brief period of fame when the BBC beamed the first public television transmission from here in 1936, but after the Second World War the palace became something of a white elephant, under-used and rather run down. In July 1980 another disastrous fire occurred, sparing only the Palm Court and the BBC section.

Public sympathy was rekindled and once again the palace was rebuilt. Nowadays the building (hopefully with more fire protection) hosts events such as a wine festival, wedding exhibition, model railway show and the London Classic Car Show. Bold plans for future developments are in the pipeline.

The terrace ends at the entrance to Palm Court (for the Phoenix bar and toilets). **Descend a grand flight of steps to Alexandra Palace Way and turn right, downhill, for 150 yards, passing steps up to The Grove car park. At a bus stop, turn right to pass a barrier and then continue ahead, gently uphill, on an avenue of limes.** There is a fenced-off 'Veteran' oak to the left, and away to the right, across the grass, is the Grove café. After cresting the hill, an island junction appears. Bear left here to **follow a covered way, then continue ahead to go through a subway under Muswell Hill.**

Now you have a choice: (A) food, drink, shops, and toilets in Muswell Hill Broadway, **or (B)** straight ahead on the Parkland Walk. Both walks link up ¼ mile further on.

(A) Go up the ramp and turn left, uphill, to a roundabout, then turn left into Muswell Hill Broadway. There are toilets located in the car park in Summerland Gardens, which is the first left turning. The popular Crocodile Garden Café is a little further along the Broadway. To rejoin the walk either retrace your route back to the Parkland Walk to avoid steps at St James's Lane, or continue to St James's Church (with its tall spire providing quite a landmark), and then turn left into St James's Lane, where you will shortly see the old railway bridge on the downhill slope. At the bridge, take the steps on the right leading up to join (B) at the Parkland Walk and turn right.

(B) Once through the subway, carry on along the level woodland path. This is a section of the Parkland Walk. Continue, soon with rooftop views alongside, to join up with (A).Keep going on this green corridor to a bridge which takes you under Muswell Hill Road.

The 'mossy spring' which, in Old English, gave Muswell Hill its name, rose in what is now Muswell Road (although the well is now built over, a small wall-plaque marks its location). This spring, or well, was on land given in the 12th century by the Bishop of London, as Lord of the Manor of Hornsey, to the nuns of the Priory of St Mary in Clerkenwell. Pilgrimages were made to the well, to visit a chapel that had been built here, sample the curative waters, and perhaps call on the well's divine powers. Hence the area became known as 'Clerkenwell Detached', and was administered by Clerkenwell parish until 1900. This was about the time of the first housing development on this 300 ft plateau, which beforehand had been woods, farms, and small private estates. Thankfully the houses and shopping parades of Muswell Hill were planned and erected with great style and quality materials, and provide a feast of Edwardian architecture.

Above: St James's Church, in the pleasant town of Muswell Hill

Opened in 1984, the Parkland Walk follows the line of a railway that used to run from Finsbury Park, then through Highgate, to Alexandra Palace. Dependent on the palace for its main passenger traffic, the line suffered mixed fortunes, with the passenger service ceasing in 1954, and eventually closed completely in 1971. At 4½ miles, it is now London's longest local nature reserve, a section of which you can enjoy on this walk.

At Muswell Hill Road a ramp leads up to an entrance on the right, by pedestrian lights, to Highgate Wood. This is Cranley Gate. Go through the gate and follow the main path as it swings to the left (signed café, toilets) and continues through trees. At a tarmac path turn right (another sign here), then at a drinking fountain bear left, still on tarmac, passing the spot where the Capital Ring long-distance path was launched in 2005. Soon you will arrive at a perfect refuelling and picnic spot, which offers a café with outdoor tables, kiosk, and toilets.

Efficiently looked after by the Corporation of London,

the ancient (pre 1600) woodland of Highgate Wood formed part of the vast Ancient Forest of Middlesex, which merited inclusion in the Domesday Book. Oak, hornbeam and holly flourish here, thanks to the wood being purchased by the Corporation in 1886 and saved from impending development.

Above: Artistry at Archway Gate

For centuries the woodland had been managed for timber production in the traditional 'coppice with standards' procedure, involving the oaks being allowed to grow to full size ('standards') to be used in buildings, ships, etc., while other trees, particularly hornbeam, were cut at the base ('coppiced') every 10–20 years to produce firewood, sticks, charcoal and smaller items. These old practices are now being used again, on a smaller scale, to regenerate the woodland.

Go past the café to face the sports ground and then turn left to the Information Hut, which is packed with an absorbing display of Highgate Wood's natural attractions. **Behind the building, turn right to follow a path through trees** with the sports ground on your right. Soon you arrive at a children's playground (toilets to the right) and a junction with a tarmac path. **Turn right on this path to emerge on Archway Road,** at Archway Gate (if you wish to catch the Tube from Highgate station, turn left for 300 yards to traffic lights at Muswell Hill Road, where you turn left and cross the road to Wood Lane, with the hidden station entrance on the right). **Your route follows Church Road, directly opposite,** which can be reached by using the pedestrian crossing on your right. **On reaching the church (All Saints, Highgate), turn left into Talbot Road.** At the top of this road you come

Left: Highgate Wood is a delightful and popular spot for recreation

to a T-junction with The Park. **Turn right here along Park House Passage, which leads to North Hill, where you turn left, uphill.**

As you progress towards Highgate Village, the surroundings hold much of interest. On the left, pop singer Rod Stewart's boyhood home was in one of the red-brick council flats of Hillcrest, while on the opposite side of North Hill are the Modernist apartment blocks of Highpoint One and Two. Quite revolutionary and controversial when they appeared in the 1930s, they were designed by Berthold Lubetkin and the Tecton Partnership, who were responsible for other well-known local authority buildings in Finsbury and elsewhere. Lubetkin was so pleased with his efforts that he built himself a penthouse on Highpoint Two. They are now Grade 1 listed, and still possess original features such as cork floors, metal doors, and concertina windows. There may be guided tours of parts of the buildings on London Open House weekend.

Back on your side of the road, the rebuilt Wrestlers pub was one of Highgate's many inns to offer travellers, before the days of the motor car, the age-old ceremony of 'Swearing on the Horns'. Somewhat tongue-in-cheek, the landlord of the inn, dressed in mask, wig, and black

The Wrestlers Tavern

"Swearing on the Horns"

This ancient ceremony dating back to 1623 is held at this tavern twice yearly in March and August.

A person swearing the oath on the horns will pay a fine which goes to charity and he will receive a certificate. The oath is displayed in full inside.

Further details and dates are obtainable from within.

Above: The story of 'swearing on the horns' at the Wrestlers in Highgate

gown, and holding a pole with a set of horns fixed to it, would greet arrivals disembarking from their coaches with various outlandish verses and promises, with the amazed traveller being required, frequently, to kiss the horns. The Wrestlers still has the horns and a sample oath to be sworn, which customers can view while enjoying a drink.

No wonder people came from far and wide to be 'sworn-in' and receive the freedom of Highgate, and no doubt to enjoy an excuse to visit some of the local hostelries. This ancient custom is still occasionally practised, nowadays for charity.

A few yards on, at number 90, Charles Dickens, with his parents and family, came in 1832 'to Mrs Goodman's, next door to the Red Lion' for a change of air.

Continue ahead, crossing Castle Yard. This is now North Road, with Highgate School a little further up on your left and an appealing array of old buildings opposite.

Several of these charming structures show signs of their commercial past, as forge, grain merchant, warehouse, or inn. Now only the Red Lion and Sun, with the petrol station nearby (which used to be the Bell and Horns inn), are reminders of the bustle and activity of days gone by. The Gatehouse inn, at the roundabout, recalls the site of an ancient toll-gate entrance to the Bishop of London's park, and still has boundary markers (on the wall facing the High Street) of the old parishes of St Pancras and St Mary's, Hornsey. It is here that you leave the London Borough of Haringey and enter Camden.

At the roundabout bear left into the centre of Highgate Village, and cross Southwood Lane at a zebra crossing. Immediately cross the High Street at another crossing and turn right to arrive opposite the end of Southwood Lane. After 30 yards descend a short flight of stone steps (or continue for a few yards to a ramp) to Pond Square and turn left. Go diagonally right across the square, under a canopy of limes and London planes. Stage One of the walk ends here.

Tree-shaded and tranquil, Pond Square is the perfect place to rest your feet. Everything you need is here; seats, toilets, pleasant surroundings, the High Street eating-places nearby, or the Village Deli for your lunchtime snack. Once rested, and if time permits, some local exploration will pay off (see the next paragraph), but if you have to finish here, there are buses from the High Street, or you may prefer an easy downhill stroll of half-a-mile to Archway station, which is on the Northern line.

For those with energy to spare, try this circular 1½ mile tour of the Highlights of Highgate. It will take about an hour, not including any time you may wish to spend visiting Highgate Cemetery, and will lead you back to Pond Square.

From Pond Square, cross to the Highgate Literary and Scientific Institution and turn left. At the Angel pub turn right along the High Street.

The High Street marks the old parish boundary between Hornsey and St Pancras. As you pass the pedestrian lights, a terrace of 18th-century town houses are on your right, including Englefield House and the dental practice at number 21. Across the road is Townsend Yard, which contains a lone survivor of a row of 17th-century dwellings, while a little further on is the Duke's Head, a former coaching inn.

Continue along the right-hand pavement of the High Street, passing Bisham Gardens.

For a greater insight into the events and characters that have shaped Highgate's history, drop into the Highgate Bookshop, on the corner of Bisham Gardens, for a selection of informative guidebooks, many of them written and produced by the Hornsey Historical Society.

As you continue downhill, passing an entrance to Waterlow Park, there are two handsome 17th-century buildings opposite; Ivy House and Northgate House. Further downhill, on The Bank, are more houses from the same period, notably cupola-topped Cromwell House, which is Grade I listed. This fine red-brick building dates from 1638 and has carved replica figures of Parliamentary soldiers on the stairs, the originals having gone missing. The High Commission of Ghana now occupies this house.

Right: Cromwell House is one of Highgate's many beautiful old houses

Back on your side of the road is a wall-plaque marking the spot where Andrew Marvell (1621–78) 'Poet, Wit, and Satirist' lived. A few yards on is Lauderdale House, where Nell Gwynn is supposed to have entertained

King Charles II. There is a café here, in a leafy parkland setting.

Carry on past Lauderdale House to a set of traffic lights. Cross Highgate Hill left at the lights to follow Hornsey Lane for ¼ mile to Archway Bridge.

While admiring the vista of the City from this spectacular viewpoint, your curiosity might make you wonder about the origins of this famous bridge, and the deep road cutting that it straddles. Imagine the rural scene here two hundred years ago, when this road did not exist; traffic, both horse-drawn and pedestrian, was obliged to labour up steep, muddy, and rutted Highgate Hill. A by-pass was needed badly, and eventually plans for a tunnel at this spot were approved, and construction work started. However, early on the morning of 13 April 1812 the part-completed tunnel collapsed, necessitating an abrupt change of plan.

With a cutting now the only option work continued apace, with John Nash, fresh from such grand architectural projects as Buckingham Palace and Regent Street, now in charge. Surprisingly for such an eminent man Nash's work proved to be defective, causing the road to be beset with problems from the day it opened. Poor surfacing and drainage led to low toll income, which meant a shortage of funds for maintenance. It was not until the turn of the 19th century when the present bridge was erected and the road widened to accommodate horse-drawn trams that matters really improved.

There are several interesting features here. The lamps at each end of the bridge are copies of those on the Embankment, designed by Lewis Vulliamy, architect of St Michael's Church in Highgate. Viewed from the cutting below, on the north side of the parapet is the crest of Middlesex, Hornsey Lane being on the old boundary with London; and there is a date of 1897 on the ironwork, marking Queen Victoria's Diamond

Above: Archway Bridge offers a breathtaking view of the City

Jubilee, although the bridge did not open until 1900. If you would like to see the bridge from below, make your way down Tile Kiln Lane (just before the bridge) from where steps lead down to the main road.

Retrace your route back to Highgate Hill, and cross at the lights to the corner of Dartmouth Park Hill.

On the opposite corner, topped by its landmark green copper dome, is St Joseph's Catholic Church, opened in 1885 with capacity for 2,000 worshippers; across the road is the Old Crown pub, built in 1898; and ¼ mile down the hill, and not included in this tour, is the Whittington Stone, where four-times Lord Mayor of London Dick Whittington (and his cat) is supposed to have heard Bow Bells calling him back to the city.

There are two well-worn stone parish boundary markers, of Islington and St Pancras, on the corner of Dartmouth Park Hill, and one for Hornsey, which is buried under the road.

Walk forward a few yards on Dartmouth Park Hill to go through a gate into Waterlow Park. Keep straight ahead on a downhill path (the café at Lauderdale House is off to the right). An open area of sloping lawn soon appears, graced with an array of comfortable-looking benches (turn left here for the Waterlow Centre, which has toilets).

179

Sir Sydney Waterlow, Lord Mayor of London 1872–73, had his private estate here. In a fine gesture of altruism, he purchased land belonging to the surrounding five houses to create these lush acres, 'a garden for the gardenless', which he presented to the London County Council in 1889.

Cross a bridge separating two ponds, then keep ahead on this wide tarmac path to eventually **leave the park through an elaborate wrought-iron and stone-pillared gate into Swain's Lane. Turn left for a few yards to Highgate Cemetery.**

Highgate's fame is based not only on the poets and monarchs who loved being here, but also on the many illustrious citizens interred in its two wooded and atmospheric Victorian burial grounds. Together the West ('Old') and East ('New') cemeteries contain over 52,000 graves, with perhaps the best-known being that of Karl Marx. Other famous individuals resting here include Frank Matcham, prolific theatre builder, responsible for over 150 theatres, often in the flamboyant style of the Hackney Empire or The Coliseum; Charles Cruft, creator of the dog show; Phillip Harben, the BBC's first TV cook; Max Wall, comedian; Charles Green, a 19th-century balloonist who achieved 527 ascents; Claudia Jones, who started the Notting Hill Carnival; and many more.

Admission to the West Cemetery is for guided tours only (£5 fee); the East Cemetery is open daily (£3), except when a funeral is in progress.

From the cemetery, **return through the wrought-iron park gates and take the first path on the left,** going uphill, and parallel with Swain's Lane. **At the tennis courts, leave the park and turn right** on Swain's Lane for 150 yards to emerge in Pond Square.

Stage Two: Highgate Village to Chalk Farm

Distance 3 miles. Intermediate distances: Parliament Hill 1 mile, Savernake Road 2 miles.

Time 2 hours.

Terrain Long, fairly steep gradients for the first two miles, all on paving or tarmac, level from then on.

Refreshments pubs, cafés, and the Village Deli in Highgate Village, café at Parliament Hill Fields (also café in Swain's Lane, just off-route), and at Chalk Farm you will find the Salvation Army and The Roundhouse both have cafés with customer toilets, plus the famous Marine Ices not only serves superb sorbets and ice cream, but has a restaurant as well.

Toilets Pond Square in Highgate Village, Merton Lane/ Highgate Ponds, Parliament Hill Fields, Chalk Farm.

Transport Fare zones 2 & 3. Archway (Tube, bus), Highgate Village (bus), Gospel Oak (train, bus), Hampstead Heath (train, bus), Chalk Farm (Tube, bus).

Best time to do the walk As with Stage One, go on a clear, bright day.

Right: A peaceful corner of Highgate's East Cemetery, in which Karl Marx is buried

Start from Pond Square, Highgate Village.

From the south side of the square, facing the Highgate Literary and Scientific Institution, **turn right to follow South Grove. Continue ahead to join Highgate West Hill at St Michael's Church.**

This little corner of Highgate has known some redoubtable characters over the years. On the left, The Old Hall, itself late 17th century, stands where Arundel House used to be, a Tudor mansion in which Elizabeth I was often entertained, and where James I spent a night in June 1624 before a day's hunting at St John's Wood. His grandson, Charles II, loved coming here, and arranged meetings on Wednesday afternoons at 3 pm for the Royal Society to conduct experiments and have discussions. On a lighter note, Charles often climbed Highgate Hill for pre-arranged meetings with the fiery Nell Gwynne; on one occasion, frustrated with Charles' refusal to give their love-child a title, she dangled the poor little boy out of a window, berating the king with 'unless you do something for him, here he goes!' Quick as a flash, Charles shot back 'save the Earl of Burford!'

Tucked away to the right is The Flask inn, its rustic appeal and snug, homely interior hard to resist. In days gone by, health-giving waters from the nearby Hampstead wells could be enjoyed from a flask provided by the inn. Across the busy road from here are the elegant, secluded houses of The Grove, 'Highgate's most desirable address', where at number 3 Samuel Taylor Coleridge lived with his friends Dr and Mrs Gillman, who helped him in his struggle with laudanum addiction, although he would secretly obtain supplies from a local chemist's shop. He lived here, his room at the back of the house enjoying views over Ken Wood, until his death in 1834. Coleridge endeared himself to the locals, and was said to be '... the finest dreamer, the most eloquent talker, and the most original thinker of his day'.

Highgate Village is over 400 ft above sea level, so it is not surprising that the handsome church of St Michael's is a notable landmark. The church was built in 1832 by two members of the Cubitt family, prolific London builders of this period. Coleridge and some of his family are buried here. As you pass the church you may notice a weather-beaten milestone which announces 'IV (4) Miles from Saint Giles Pound'; the 'I' was added by some mischief-maker, the 'V' (5) being the true figure, important to religious non-conformists who at one time were not allowed to practice within five miles of the City.

On the opposite side of the road are two locked gates, behind which is Witanhurst, said to be London's largest private residence after Buckingham Palace. It was constructed 1913–17 around an older house for Sir Arthur Crosfield, Sunlight Soap magnate, and his socialite wife, Domini. Splendid pre-Wimbledon tennis parties were held in the seven acres of gardens, and in more recent times the BBC talent show Fame Academy was filmed here.

Stay on the left-hand pavement as you continue walking down Highgate West Hill, and then turn right at Merton Lane, taking care to cross at the refuge. This lane ends opposite a barrier entrance to Hampstead Heath. **Weave your way round the barrier** (there are toilets on the right) and follow the tarmac path on a gentle downhill slope.

Go straight ahead between two of Highgate's ponds and then bear left with the boating (and fishing) pond on your left. Where this pond ends continue ahead to a junction of paths, with Highgate men's bathing pond (£2 if you fancy a dip) screened by trees. **Pass the first junction, and then go ahead under two London plane trees to then bear right, uphill,** on a no-cycling path which, on nearing the hilltop, snakes through a copse of mature trees. Once clear of the trees, bear left across grass on a well-worn track to scale the last few feet to the 320 ft summit of Parliament Hill.

How Parliament Hill got its name is a matter of some doubt, although one appealing theory concerns Guy Fawkes and his fellow conspirators who hoped to watch the results of their gunpowder plot against Parliament in 1605 from here. Nowadays people come to fly kites, and enjoy the fresh air and scenery, which includes, amongst Highgate's wooded slopes, the green dome of St Joseph's Catholic Church, the spire of St Anne's at the foot of West Hill, and St Michael's on its hilltop site. Farther afield are the distinctive towers and spires of the City of London and Canary Wharf, awash in a great metropolitan sea.

From the grassy track, at the summit seats, **turn left to follow the downhill path, with more of Highgate's ponds on the left below you.** Keep ahead on this path, ignoring side turnings, to descend through more trees and finally arrive at a café (right) and toilets (left).

These facilities are situated between a bandstand and an immaculate, flower-bordered bowling green. In common with Highgate Wood and many other green

spaces in and around London, Parliament Hill Fields
are extremely well looked after by the Corporation of
London for the public to enjoy. If you wish to digress
from the walk, there is an exit to Highgate Road at this
point, where a left turn leads directly to a bus stop, pub,
café, and shops in Swain's Lane. The white-painted
obelisk that you will have walked past on the downhill
path is the Stone of Free Speech, where in bygone days
open-air public meetings were held.

To continue your walk, **at the café and toilets
turn right and press on along a wide
path with an athletics track on your left.**
Soon you reach a pavilion (toilets here), children's
playground, and paddling pool, after which you bear
left to **leave Parliament Hill Fields by way of
a footbridge** which crosses the North London line
and emerges on Savernake Road (there are two railway
stations nearby; turn left here for Gospel Oak, or right
for Hampstead Heath). Cross slightly left to **carry on
along Roderick Road.** At the end of this road
**turn right then cross left at the lights to
continue along Southampton Road.** When
the road bears left, use the crossing to gain the right-

hand pavement on which you stay to bear right, still on Southampton Road, passing the ornate front of St Dominic's Priory.

Keep on ahead, now on Maitland Park Villas, with high hedges hiding a pleasant lawned square around which are grouped the St Pancras Almshouses. Soon Maitland Park Road, as it has now become, ends at Prince of Wales Road. **Cross this road at the lights** and maintain your direction as you descend the gentle slope of Haverstock Hill to **then cross right at the lights to Chalk Farm station**, in Adelaide Road, and the end of Stage Two. The Roundhouse, which is just a few yards off your route, is mentioned in Stage Three.

Left: This bridge leads to the individual shops and cafés of Primrose Hill

Stage Three: Chalk Farm to Little Venice

Distance 3 Miles. Intermediate distances: Primrose Hill Bridge 1 mile, Lisson Grove 2 miles.

Time 2 hours.

Terrain A steep climb to Primrose Hill on tarmac paths, then a section of   towpath between Park Road and Maida Vale with a very uneven surface and some steep steps, avoided by a detour along St John's Wood Road.

Refreshments Cafés in Chalk Farm mentioned in Stage Two, plenty of choice in Regent's Park Road, and St John's Wood High Street (just off route). Warwick Avenue offers some choice, and there is the Waterside café at Little Venice.

Toilets Chalk Farm if you are using one of the cafés, Primrose Hill, Wellington Place (just off route), Warwick Avenue.

Transport Fare zones 1 & 2. Chalk Farm (Tube, bus), Warwick Avenue (Tube, bus), Paddington (Tube, train, bus).

Best time to do the walk This is a delightful section, best enjoyed on a warm, clear day.

Right: Emerging from the Maida Hill Tunnel on the Regent's Canal

Start from Chalk Farm station (Northern line). **Turn right on Adelaide Road, then left into Bridge Approach.** Go over the wide railway bridge, high above the comings and goings of Euston station.

Chalk Farm derived its name not from the local subsoil but from the Chalcots Estate, which had been owned by Eton College since the 15th century. Chalcot in Old English means 'cold cottage' or 'cold hut'. Chalcot Farm became Chalk House Farm, which had an ale-house attached. Over the years this venture grew to be the popular Chalk House Tavern and Tea Rooms.

Until housing developers and railway engineers started a dramatic process of change from about 1830 onwards, the surroundings here were mostly farmland, with few buildings. The Regent's Canal had arrived some years earlier, opening to Islington by 1820, so the railway companies approaching from the north had to resolve whether to go over or under the canal when laying the lines to their various London termini. The London and Birmingham Railway decided to bridge the canal with their line into Euston, necessitating a slope so steep that trains had to be hauled out of the station by means of a cable as far as the Camden goods yard, not far from here.

The Roundhouse, which is slightly off your route, was part of this railway complex. It started life as an engine shed, became redundant as engines got bigger, then for many years was a warehouse for Gilbey's huge wines and spirits business based here, next to Camden goods yard.

Gilbey's left in 1963, and the building found a new use as a thriving theatre and arts centre. This project eventually ran out of funds and closed in 1984, and decay set in. Thankfully in 1996 the by-then derelict structure was purchased by a local buyer with the funds and vision to offer the Roundhouse a bright future, and now it is once more a much-loved music and arts venue.

From the railway bridge, **cross Gloucester Avenue at the refuge to continue ahead on Regent's Park Road.**

This is Primrose Hill's 'High Street', and it possesses a most interesting collection of shops and eating places, including Trojka, a Russian tearoom with a tempting menu (borsch, goulash, caviar, etc.), another shop selling pots, pans and everything for your kitchen, and Fitzroy's charming little florist's shop, by Mayfair Mews. Across the road are a pet shop, wholefood emporium, and the friendly and helpful Primrose Hill Bookshop. You will have already passed the Pembroke pub, while further on is The Queens, where real-ale fans can enjoy a pint of Young's.

Now your walk diverts briefly through some pastel-hued side streets.

After passing all the shops **take the second left into Chalcot Crescent,** which soon joins Chalcot Square. Here you will find a tree-shaded spot to sit and refresh. **Turn right to follow Chalcot Road to its junction with Fitzroy Road.**

On the left is the Princess of Wales pub, opposite which is Clare's Kitchen, a good place to buy your lunch.

Turn right to follow Fitzroy Road, and at the end **cross and go through a gate to enter Primrose Hill Park. Turn right and follow the tarmac path to the summit,** 206 ft above sea level.

Primrose Hill was saved as a park by an Act of Parliament of 1842, after various development threats had been averted, notably a scheme to tunnel into the hill and construct a huge mausoleum with room for five million coffins. The London skyline is much more close-up from here; in fact the view of St Paul's is protected by statute, and cannot be spoilt or obscured. The Post Office Tower seems larger than life, and the London Eye and Houses of Parliament stand out clearly. A few small boundary markers are dotted about on the hillside, denoting the old parishes of St Pancras, St Marylebone, and St John, Hampstead, which met on these slopes. One small iron marker boldly announces 'St PP [St Pancras Parish] 1821'.

From the circular brick-inset hilltop, **continue ahead on the downhill path,** which gently curves to the left. At a junction of paths (for toilets, take the third path on the left) continue ahead to the exit. **Cross Prince Albert Road, turn right and then immediately left** towards Primrose Hill Bridge and the Regent's Canal. **Just before the bridge turn right** on a path which soon curves sharply left round a hairpin bend to **join the canal towpath, where you turn right.**

The Regent's Canal came into being from 1812, being completed in stages from Paddington to Limehouse, serving London's docks and also the many wharves and basins along the way. It wasn't long before the railways arrived and brought fierce competition, but at this time London was enlarging dramatically, so bricks, sand, coal, hay and straw, and other bulk goods kept the canal busy for many years. Pickford's was one of the most successful canal carrying companies, offering a fast boat service to Birmingham, with the towing horses, which were changed regularly, proceeding at a trot. This cut the journey time from 4 to 2½ days.

Press on along the towpath, with the canal and Regent's Park on your left. Soon you will arrive at Macclesfield, or 'Blow-up', bridge.

Early one morning in October 1874 there was a terrific explosion here. Five barges, containing amongst other goods petroleum and five tons of gunpowder, were being towed along by a tug on their journey to the Midlands. No-one knows why, but this dangerous cargo exploded, demolishing the bridge and a gas main, and causing panic among the animals in London Zoo, not to mention the local population. There was a suggestion that one of the three crew members, none of whom survived, may have been smoking, and had just knocked the ashes out of his pipe. When the bridge was rebuilt, the cast-iron bridge supports were re-used, but turned round so that the tow-rope grooves now face away from the water.

Left: Primrose Hill's grassy slopes are a perfect picnic spot

Continue along the towpath, passing under Charlbert Bridge. If you wish to take advantage of the cafés in St John's Wood, or the toilets in Wellington Place (open 10:00–18:00), leave the canalside here and cross Prince Albert Road. Turn left, then take the second right into St John's Wood High Street. Wellington Place is at the end of the church gardens on the left. You can rejoin the canal at Park Road, opposite the mosque, using the crossing by Lodge Road.

The Canal and Regent's Park were named in honour of the Prince Regent, who was to become George IV, when they were developed between 1812–20 by John Nash, a famous and fashionable architect of the time. The idea was to fill the park with villas (such as those visible here) for the great and good but concerns were raised about the need for more public recreational space, and Nash's grand scheme was, thankfully, never completed.

Looking across the water, you may notice the minaret and copper-domed roof of the London Central Mosque behind some grand villas.

The towpath takes you, in quick succession, under Park Road, then two railway bridges (Tube trains

191

first, then the Chiltern line), and then a footbridge to the Lisson Green Estate. **Just keep going along the waterside, or divert to St John's Wood Road to avoid the uneven towpath and steep steps ahead.**

Now the canal broadens to provide space for a tightly packed terrace of narrow-boat homes with adjacent gardens, pot-plants, bags of coal, bicycles, and all the trappings of permanent residence. Beware of the 'speed-humps' here, which help to enforce the no-cycling rule on this stretch. This watery hamlet is known as Lisson Broad.

Once past the houseboats, your towpath walk continues through a short tunnel under Lisson Grove (it's low; **mind your head**) and then swings left towards the Maida Hill Tunnel, which has no towpath.

In the days of horse-power, before towing tugs were introduced, this tunnel and the much longer Islington Tunnel had to be 'legged through', because there was no towing-path. Sometimes this was done by professional 'leggers', lying on their backs on a rigged-up plank fixed to the barge, and pushing their way along the damp tunnel walls. The towing horses would be led over the top, which must at least have given them a break, to then meet the boat as it emerged.

The Maida Hill Tunnel is 272 yards long and boats must wait their turn to enter this narrow waterway. You can literally 'see a light at the end of the tunnel' when a boat is approaching.

Climb the steps and go ahead through a barrier to emerge in Aberdeen Place, which you follow straight ahead.

Victorian pub architecture at its most flamboyant is on display at Crocker's Folly, Aberdeen Place. Completed in 1899, this lavish hotel-cum-pub was built for Frank Crocker, a well-known local character. He was convinced that the Great Central Railway would site its terminus here, but in the event Marylebone was chosen, leaving his pub out on a limb. It survived in spite of these difficulties, but at the time of writing it lies unused.

Cross Maida Vale at pedestrian lights and continue ahead on Blomfield Road, passing a restaurant perched high above the re-emerged canal.

Now Little Venice shows off in great style; waterside trees and gardens provide a colourful addition to the bright array of houseboats, while the grandiose, white-stucco Victorian mansions create the perfect backdrop.

Just before the traffic lights at Warwick Avenue, go down a short ramp to follow alongside the canal again, passing under the first of several bright blue bridges (for toilets, go across the bridge and continue to Rembrandt Gardens, on the right. For Warwick Avenue station and the Warwick Castle pub in Warwick Place, turn right at the traffic lights).

Left: Chugging along to Lisson Broad

The cheerful scene that greets you now belies the former importance of this junction of the Regent's and Grand Union canals. Before road and rail took over, goods from all over the country, as well as imports from London's docks, would have passed this way, progressing slowly to and from the industrial Midlands and North.

Carry on along the water's edge **to cross the canal at Westbourne Terrace Road,** with the Waterside café conveniently placed by the bridge. This is the end of Stage Three of the Peaks and Troughs walk. For Paddington rail and Tube stations and Praed Street, where there are plenty of pubs, cafés, and also bus services, continue on the well-signposted waterside towards Paddington Basin. Stage Four of your walk turns left to go under the bridge.

Stage Four: Little Venice to Notting Hill

Distance 3 miles. Intermediate distances: Great Western Road 1 mile, Portobello Road (at the Westway) 2 miles.

Time 2 hours.

Terrain Fairly level canal towpath, pavement.

Refreshments Waterside cafés at Paddington Basin and Little Venice, the canalside Grand Union pub at Great Western Road, and numerous establishments of every description in Golborne and Portobello Roads, and at Notting Hill.

Toilets Rembrandt Gardens, Warwick Avenue; Golborne Road, Portobello Road, Notting Hill Gate.

Transport Fare zones 1 & 2. Paddington (Tube, train, bus), Warwick Avenue (Tube, bus), Westbourne Park (Tube, bus), Ladbroke Grove (Tube, bus), Notting Hill Gate (Tube, bus).

Best time to do the walk Saturday for Portobello Road market, or anytime for an enjoyable walk.

Left: A place to relax before tackling the last stage of your walk

Start at Little Venice, by the Waterside café next to the canal bridge at Westbourne Terrace Road.

This triangle of water, also known as Browning's Pool and Island, after the poet Robert Browning who lived nearby from 1862 to 1887, is the venue for the annual Canalway Cavalcade. Held over the Mayday Bank Holiday, it is a boater's rally and beanfeast which features boat-handling competitions, children's entertainments, and a procession of illuminated boats. Along with a jazz band, sideshows, guided walks, and real-ale bar, this three-day event is a unique treat. Also on offer here, year round, are boat trips to Camden Lock and London Zoo.

Pass the café, go under the bridge, and continue along the towpath, with a line of houseboats for company, and Delamere Terrace to your left. You are now following the Paddington Arm of the Grand Union Canal.

Soon, on your left, the sombre red-brick exterior of St Mary Magdalene's Church hides a richly decorated interior which has been much used for TV and films, from *The Blue Lamp* with Dirk Bogarde and Jack Warner to a more recent filming of *The Oxford Murders* starring Elijah Wood. A little further on, an eye-catching and colourful piece of wall-art, created from litter, enlivens the canal scene.

Carry on along the towpath to go under Harrow Road Bridge before converging with the A40 Westway, which fortunately is a safe distance overhead.

Above and beside you are the rival routes that between them stole the canal's trade. Improved roads and railways slowly took more and more business away, until a bitterly cold winter in 1962–3 froze the canals for three months, causing the remaining customers to go elsewhere, never to return. That's when leisure boating took over.

Part of the canal's attraction here is that you cannot see the traffic or trains that are so close by. An accelerating Inter-City express can sometimes be heard, and the Westway's hum is always there, but the peaceful waters by your side seem to absorb most of the noise, while your leisurely pace is set by the occasional narrowboat chugging slowly past. Now and then a coot or moorhen may disturb the peace, chasing off an interloper.

Continue under the next bridge at Great Western Road (for Westbourne Park station, go up spiral steps to the road and turn right). Now you find yourself walking alongside Meanwhile Gardens, with some neat tree-clipping to admire across the canal. When you come to a modern waterside terrace of red-pillared dwellings on the other side of the canal, bid farewell to this pleasant waterway, **and leave the towpath to go down a ramp signed for Golborne Road and Portobello Market. Continue ahead to follow Golborne Road.**

Now you pass the gigantic 31 storey Trellick Tower, hailed as something of a novelty when built in the late 1960s as included in the design were an old people's club, nursery, a shopping arcade, and even a bank. The lift-shaft is detached from the building to reduce noise for the residents. Trellick Tower and Balfron Tower, its slightly smaller sister in east London, were designed by a man with the splendid name of Erno Goldfinger. On a sunny day, viewed from a distance, with washing flapping from every balcony, it resembles a vast clothes line. Goldfinger was a well-known and accomplished architect who lived in Hampstead, but apparently did not get on with one of his neighbours, the James Bond author Ian Fleming. Perhaps this was the inspiration for one of Fleming's arch-villains.

Carry on over the railway bridge, crossing the Great Western tracks in and out of Paddington. Golborne Road continues, with an eclectic mixture of shops and stalls, to a junction with Portobello Road (there are toilets on the left, in Bevington Road). **Turn left to follow Portobello Road** on its long southward course, which will take you under the Westway at Portobello Green (this is the place to turn right if you wish to go to Ladbroke Grove station).

Left: Trellick Tower presents a striking sight for miles around

There is much of interest as you wend your way through the hurly-burly; look out for a huge, gleaming, wall-size mosaic, 'Echoes of Spain 1936–1939' which brightens the scene beneath the Westway, and once across Westbourne Park Road, some traditional 'costermongers' fruit and vegetable stalls, adding their contribution to the market aroma. The shops here range from basic to quirky, and literary; a quick eyes-right when passing Blenheim Crescent will reveal a nest of bookshops, including Garden Books, full of interest for the green-fingered; Books for Cooks, where they test the recipes on the customers; and the Travel Bookshop, a great source of information for would-be globetrotters, and the inspiration for Hugh Grant's bookshop in 'Notting Hill'.

Moving on, there is the Electric Cinema, possibly England's oldest purpose-built cinema, dating from 1910, with a handsome front bedecked with swags of flowers and fruit; and several pubs, including the Duke of Wellington, a Young's pub. Every now and then an enclave of bright little mews cottages appears, and as you progress, the antique shops hold sway.

Portobello's busy day is Saturday, when the antique and

flea market takes over, but there is also a half-market on Friday. During the week the fruit and vegetable stalls are lively, with an organic section under the canopy by the Westway on Thursday, which is early closing day for some stalls in the main market. At any time of the week, though, this famous road is fascinating; the absolute antidote to so many 'clone' high streets.

Left: Portobello Road wouldn't be the same without fascinating shops such as Alice's

Press on along Portobello Road (there are toilets on the way, at the junctions with Tavistock Road, Talbot Road, and then Lonsdale Road).

Notting Hill had its problems in the 1950s: racial tensions that led to riots, seedy housing and greedy landlords, and a few years later, destruction caused by the Westway. Fifty years on there is Carnival, attracting two million party-goers over the August Bank Holiday; a red-hot property market; and a film, called simply Notting Hill, with Hugh Grant and Julia Roberts giving the area a boost. It all adds up to one of London's most desirable and appealing 'villages'.

Your final ascent begins now as you **cross Westbourne Grove and then Chepstow**

Villas to continue on a much-narrowed Portobello Road. Now you pass a shop selling an incredible range of tinplate signs and souvenirs.

Across the road is St Peter's Church Hall, home to the delightful Charlie's Café, welcoming its customers through a courtyard draped with greenery into a homely interior, ranged with well-worn wooden tables and chairs, where the good food and friendly service will revive the weary walker or the frazzled bargain-hunter.

Below: Cabman's halt – the taxi drivers' shelter in Kensington Park Road

The market is left behind as you wend your way past a smart terrace of cottages, after which **a sharp left-hand bend brings you to a T-junction with Pembridge Road,** with the Sun in Splendour pub on the corner. Turn right here, and use one of the zebra crossings to continue your journey on the left-hand pavement to meet Notting Hill Gate. The Tube station can be found just a few yards along on the left (there is a toilet 100 yards to the right).

This is where the curtain comes down on the Peaks and Troughs walk, the end of Stage Four. For refreshment,

on the other side of the main road, behind the Coronet Cinema with its frivolous Victorian façade, are several streets of colourful terraced cottages which have in their midst the Hillgate pub in Hillgate Street, and the Uxbridge Arms in Uxbridge Street, both of which are appealing watering holes. For less exotic surroundings the green taxi drivers' shelter in Kensington Park Road offers a variety of victuals, served through a hatch. What more could you ask for? Treat yourself to something special; you've earned it after all that foot-slogging.

9 Village Life

Deptford to Brixton in three stages

Conjuring up a mental picture of rural bliss in some rustic, unhurried English village scene is not an easy task amidst the helter-skelter traffic and cosmopolitan surroundings of a typical south London street; a casual visitor could be forgiven for thinking that it has always been this way, but the reality is that a sprinkling of modest Surrey hamlets, some of which had been quite contented in their verdant isolation since Domesday, were swiftly engulfed by prolific Victorian terrace-builders in the unbridled 19th-century expansion of the capital.

Starting from the cheerfully old-fashioned village of Deptford, with its lively street market, this walk visits well-known centres that are bustling and thriving, and a few that are by-passed by the throng, until you reach your final goal amongst the flamboyant buildings, busy markets, and tumult of activity that is 21st-century Brixton.

Stage One: Deptford to Peckham Rye

Distance 5½ miles. Intermediate distances: Deptford Creek 1 mile, Albany Arts Centre 2 miles, New Cross Gate 3 miles, Nunhead station 4 miles.

Time 3½ hours.

Terrain All paving or tarmac, with steep gradients at Pepys Road and Telegraph Hill Park.

Refreshments Just about everything you could desire in Deptford, from FairTrade organic to pie and mash. Some choice in New Cross, several pubs and the Crossways Café in Nunhead, and a limited selection in Peckham.

Toilets Deptford, Telegraph Hill, and Rye Lane, Peckham.

Transport Fare zones 2 & 3. Deptford Bridge (DLR, bus), Deptford (train), New Cross (train, bus), New Cross Gate (train, bus), Nunhead (train, bus), Peckham Rye (train, bus). The East London line is re-opening in 2010.

Best time to do the walk On Wednesday, Friday, or Saturday, Deptford's market days.

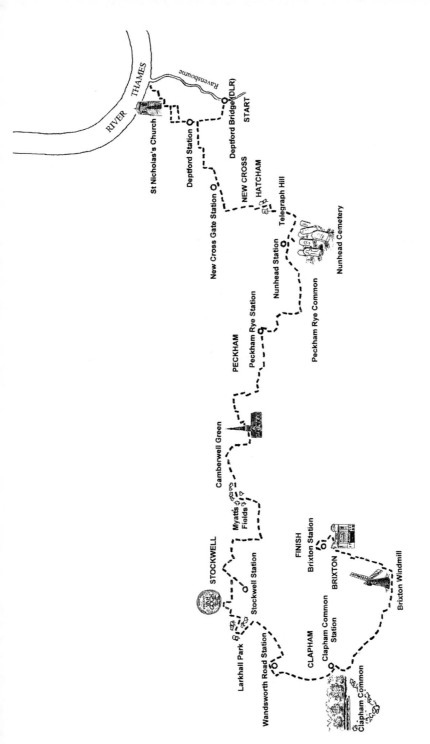

RIVER THAMES

Ravensbourne

St Nicholas's Church

Deptford Station

Deptford Bridge (DLR)
START

New Cross Gate Station

NEW CROSS

HATCHAM

Telegraph Hill

Nunhead Station

Nunhead Cemetery

Peckham Rye Common

PECKHAM

Peckham Rye Station

Camberwell Green

Myatt's Fields

STOCKWELL

Stockwell Station

Larkhall Park

Wandsworth Road Station

CLAPHAM

Clapham Common Station

Clapham Common

FINISH

Brixton Station

BRIXTON

Brixton Windmill

D eptford derived its name from the 'Deep Ford' across the River Ravensbourne, which was first mentioned in 1345. There is a suggestion that a bridge existed long before this, built by the Romans on their road from London to Canterbury and Dover. The ford must have been crossed by many a crusader, pilgrim, or monk on their way southwards.

Start at Deptford Bridge station (DLR trains to Lewisham, Bank, and Stratford).From the station platforms high above Deptford Bridge, **take the exit for Lewisham College** (there is a lift at the other end of the platforms). Descend to street level, **turn right, and cross the River Ravensbourne, heading for Deptford Broadway.**

Deptford owes much to the Ravensbourne. At its junction with the mighty Thames it forms Deptford Creek, part of the area chosen by King Henry VIII in 1513 as the site for his new naval dockyard. For centuries the dockyard prospered, turning Deptford from a fishing village into a town, and remaining active until 1869.

Elizabeth I visited Captain Drake after his round-the-world voyage, knighted him, and dined with him aboard the Golden Hind while the ship was moored in Deptford Creek. Remaining tied-up for some years, this once-fine ship eventually fell to bits, leaving just enough timber to make a chair, which ended up in Oxford.

Walk past Lewisham College, cross the wide thoroughfare of Deptford Church Street with care, and after 150 yards **turn right to follow the High Street through the market area.**

Almost opposite the end of the High Street and slightly off your route is Tanner's Hill, where there are some very old shops, notably Witcomb Hand-Built Cycles, and W H Wellbeloved Butchers, established in 1829.

Above: St Paul's Church stands as a testament to the talents of architect Thomas Archer

Pass the Deptford Arms and the junction of Giffin Street and Douglas Way (there are toilets to the right in Giffin Street, across the paved area). **Continue ahead under the railway bridge** at Deptford station (which was opened in 1836, and is said to be London's oldest working station). 100 yards after the bridge, **turn right to enter St Paul's Churchyard,** on Diamond Way. Carry on along a tarmac path with the church on your right.

St Paul's Church was designed by Thomas Archer, an architect who had worked with Wren and Hawksmoor, and who was also responsible for St John, Smith Square, Westminster. Consecrated in 1730 as Deptford's new parish church, the massive Tuscan columns of the entrance portico, combined with the graceful tower and spire and the imposing flights of steps on each side of the building, are still awe-inspiring in this workaday locality. If the church is open, do go in; the interior is spectacular.

Leave the churchyard through a gate onto Deptford Church Street. Turn left and continue to the traffic lights at the junction with Creek Road. Take note of a pathway on the left here; you will be going that way later, as you will return to this point after visiting the Thames riverside at Deptford Creek.

Your route now lies straight ahead to Deptford Green, a side road to the left of the modern block of flats on the opposite side of Creek Road, which involves crossing **right at these lights, then left,** with the green man to guide you across this busy junction. Once safely on the other side, go ahead on the side road for 100 yards, passing McMillan Street on the left, to arrive at the historic parish church of St Nicholas. Although your route lies straight ahead through the churchyard, it is not a right of way, so a short diversion around the churchyard wall is necessary.

Dedicated to the patron saint of seafarers, the ancient church of St Nicholas at one time had Trinity House, which was set up in the 16th century to oversee Britain's lighthouses, as a next door neighbour. Being so close to the naval dockyard and the Thames, it is no surprise that the church contains several centuries-old monuments to mariners and shipwrights. The weather-worn skull and crossbones on each gatepost may have been the inspiration for the pirate's Jolly Roger flag, but the carvings also contain laurel wreaths, a sign of immortality. Elizabethan poet and playwright Christopher Marlowe, said to have been killed in a dispute over a lodging-house bill in 1593, is probably the churchyard's most famous occupant. A tablet on the far wall marks his burial spot.

Above: Skull-topped gateposts mark the entrance to historic St Nicholas's Church

Superb wood-carver Grinling Gibbons, who lived in a solitary house nearby, was 'discovered' by John Evelyn in 1671, when curiosity made him peep into Gibbon's window and see him at work. Through John Evelyn's influence, Grinling Gibbons met Sir Christopher Wren, and went on to adorn many a church and chapel with his crisp and skilful work. Some fine carving in St Nicholas's is attributed to him, or his craftsmen.

This church has great age, and has survived against the odds. Most of the tower dates from the 14th century, and the main body of the building from 1697–98. An incendiary bomb caused dreadful damage in World War Two, and then vandals did their best to complete the destruction, but happily the church was rebuilt in 1956–58. It is normally open Wed–Sat 9.30–12.30.

Turn right to follow a narrow street that goes by the name of Stowage, alongside the churchyard wall. Where this wall ends, **turn left through a gated entrance** to numbers 20–42 Stowage and **then bear right to go through a gate in the centre of a crescent of small, modern houses**. Once through the gate, go straight ahead through a modern estate, at first by a car park, then along Marlowe Path, aiming for an archway in the far block of flats. Your goal is just the other side of this archway, which unfortunately is private, so **on emerging from Marlowe Path turn left and continue on Glaisher Street to the riverside, where a right turn leads you swiftly to the mouth of Deptford Creek.**

Right: The future Czar Peter the Great, 6'2" tall, flanked by his dwarf, an armchair, and canons

This is where Thames and Ravensbourne meet. Greenwich and its domed foot-tunnel entrance buildings are included in the broad downstream vista. Giving the waterside scene an added twist is a strangely compelling statue of Peter the Great, Czar of Russia, surveying the riverside from a raised platform. On his right is an ornate armchair, and to the left his companion dwarf, in jolly mood, there to accentuate his master's tall stature.

Peter spent four months in Deptford in 1698, studying shipbuilding at the dockyard. He rented Sayes Court, the home of John Evelyn, who was horrified to find his beautiful house and cherished gardens much abused after Peter's stay, with torn fabrics, spattered walls, and pictures that had been used for target practice. The house was pulled down about thirty years later, but is still remembered in Sayes Court Park. John Evelyn's fellow 17th-century diarist, Samuel Pepys, visited Deptford often in his capacity as Clerk to the Navy Board. He would come, usually 'by water', to sort out problems and issue instructions at the dockyard, frequently calling at Greenwich and Woolwich as well.

Now retrace your steps back through the estate, away from the river, past St Nicholas Church, across Creek Road and Deptford Church Street, to take the pathway by the traffic lights that you noted earlier, which leads to Albury Street.

Cherubs, winged angels, acanthus leaves, fruit, nautical charts and dividers adorn the carved doorways of Albury Street. Built for naval officers and ship's captains, these rare houses date from 1707–15.

Continue along Albury Street to make acquaintance once more with Deptford High Street. **Turn left and go back under the railway bridge,** then take the **first right to follow Douglas Way**, through the flea-market area and past the Albany arts and community centre (toilets and café here).

Right: The tangled maze that tops Goldsmith's College is quite a sight in the evening sun

On market days Douglas Way is home to a startling array of second-hand goods, ranging from creaky old tables and chairs to battered suitcases and the odd shoe, and anything else that springs to mind in between. On one extensive stall, a redoubtable, sharp-eyed lady conducts proceedings perched on a crate on top of her stall, or sometimes from the top of a step-ladder.

Cross Watsons Street and keep going in the same direction **through Margaret McMillan Park.**

This pleasant strip of greenery commemorates a lady who, with her sister Rachel, began an open-air nursery in Deptford in the early 1900s, and campaigned for better healthcare, food, and education for local children, many of whom suffered dreadful living conditions.

Continue through the park to the end of Douglas Way at a T-junction with Amersham Vale (turn left here for New Cross station). Cross this road, **turn left then immediately right, to go through a subway** under the railway. **Cross Pagnell Street and go through a gate into Fordham Park.** Bear left to follow the tarmac perimeter path all the way to Clifton Rise, where you turn left, uphill, to **emerge by the New Cross Inn. Turn right to follow New Cross Road.**

Take a look across the road at the old Deptford Town Hall, built in 1905 in the Baroque style, and richly embellished with nautical designs and larger than life figures of famous seafarers. Atop the clock tower is a jaunty sailing-ship weathervane. Goldsmith's College,

now part of the University of London, occupies this and several other buildings here, including a modern block behind the Town Hall, the Ben Pimlott Building, topped with a colossal, tangled piece of sculpture, which can look quite fantastic in the evening sun.

Continue for 300 yards to New Cross Gate station. Cross at the pedestrian lights to keep going in the same direction, now on the left-hand pavement. Carry on past New Cross bus garage then turn left at Pepys Road, with one or two pubs and cafés in New Cross Road, over to the right.

Previously part of the extensive Manor of Hatcham, New Cross Gate was named after the turnpike toll-gate that stood here from the early 1700s, which in turn had got its name from the New Cross or Golden Cross Inn, one of three or four inns nearby serving travellers on this important route south. Although the toll-gates were removed in 1865, the name stuck, and the centuries-old title of Hatcham now takes a bit of finding. It is still there if you search for it, in a few road names, a little park, a college, and the hilltop church of St Catherine's.

In 1614 The Haberdashers' Company bought a great deal of this land, shrewdly allowing it to be developed during the 19th-century house-building boom, with the area that you are about to walk through being earmarked for quality houses to appeal to the 'middle classes'. Two schools, built using funds endowed by Robert Aske, Master of The Haberdashers' Company in the late 17th century, were added to the estate.

Follow wide, tree-lined Pepys Road on its gradual uphill course, passing solidly made dwellings with names such as 'St Hilary', 'Gresham House', and 'Egremont'. Just before the crest of the hill, **cross right at Arbuthnot Road and go through a gate into Telegraph Hill Lower Park.**

Bear left through the park, maintaining the same uphill direction. To your right the ground slopes away to a pond, beside which is a toilet. This well-tended little green space won a Green Flag award in 2007/8. Keep bearing left to **leave through a gate** by a roundabout junction of five ways, occupied by Haberdashers' Aske's Hatcham College and St Catherine's Church. **Turn right along Kitto Road,** then after 100 yards **turn left into Telegraph Hill Upper Park.** Go steeply ahead to pass the tennis courts on your right.

Plow'd Garlic Hill, once part of a fertile produce-growing district, became Telegraph Hill after the Admiralty erected a semaphore station at the Upper Park in 1795. This was said to be the last link in the line of communication from where news of Wellington's victory at Waterloo was received in London.

Once you are past the tennis courts, an outstanding view presents itself: the Houses of Parliament, London Eye, Battersea Power Station, and on a clear day even the Wembley Arch are visible from this 160 ft summit, one of the highest points on the whole walk.

Take the right-hand path, going downhill, to **leave the park through a gate onto Drakefell Road. Cross straight over to Aspinall Road,** leading to a footbridge over a railway line, which you cross and then **turn right on St Asaph Road.** This leads over more railway lines to arrive at a double mini roundabout.

The choice now is either to continue on the main walk, or take an optional diversion to Nunhead Cemetery, which enjoys the status of a Local Nature Reserve and a Site of Metropolitan Importance for wildlife. Reckoned to be one of London's wildest habitats, it was opened along with several other out-of-town cemeteries when the City had no more room for burials. Established in 1840, it contains several buildings of interest, and regular conducted tours are held. The cemetery is normally open to the public from 08:30, and a stroll along the main avenue to the 200 ft hilltop, passing a cheerful collection of toppling obelisks and tombstones on the way, is a delight.

To visit Nunhead Cemetery, turn left at the second mini roundabout and follow Linden Grove for 300 yards to the entrance gate.

For the main walk, keep on ahead at the mini roundabouts, now on Oakdale Road, to a T-junction with Gibbon Road, at Nunhead station. **Turn left, then bear right to follow**

Kimberley Avenue, passing a sign proclaiming the presence of the Railway Tavern, which unfortunately has been replaced by flats. Press on ahead to a main road junction by the Crossways Café, then **turn left to continue along Evelina Road.**

There is some of the feeling of an old-fashioned village street here; butcher, baker, fishmonger, florist, and a little further on three pubs, one of which recalls Brock's Fireworks, which were made nearby. This famous firm's products were used for displays at the Crystal Palace.

At the end of the shopping parade **cross right at the lights to Nunhead Green** and the Pyrotechnist's Arms. Walk along the green by a row of old cottages and former almshouses. Nunhead Library, located a few yards down Gordon Road, has public toilets (closed Wednesday and Sunday). At the end of the green, by the Old Nun's Head pub, is an entrance to **Scylla Road, which you follow to cross Consort Road.**

Just to your right in Consort Road are Beeston's Gift Almshouses, built in 1834 in memory of Cuthbert Beeston, 16th-century Master of the Worshipful Company of Girdlers. There are more almshouses provided by the Girdler's Company to be seen a little later on in the walk.

At a junction of roads, **by Rye Oak Primary School, bear right,** still on Scylla Road, which you follow to a T-junction.

To your left, Peckham Rye Common spreads out, a centuries-old open space through which the River Peck once flowed. Threatened by building development planned by the lord of the manor in the 1860s, the Camberwell Vestry bought the manorial rights here and at Nunhead to preserve the area for public enjoyment. The Rye, as it was known, became such a popular place for recreation as the town expanded in the 19th century that on Bank Holidays and at weekends it was sometimes dangerously overcrowded with fun-seeking locals. Next to The Rye was Homestall Farm, which was purchased and opened as Peckham Rye Park in 1894, increasing the total area to 113 acres.

Turn right and keep going along Peckham Rye, which becomes Rye Lane at the end of the central strip of grass. **Cross Heaton Road** by the Nag's Head pub, and then **bear left to continue along the busy shopping street of Rye Lane.** After 150 yards, opposite Atwell Road (there is an automatic toilet here), cross Rye Lane and **turn left along Choumert Road,** passing an interesting variety of African and Asian shops and stalls. Finally the shops peter out at Girdler's Cottages Almshouses, where you **turn right to follow Choumert Grove.**

After 25 yards, peep through a gate on the right to catch a glimpse of the private, unspoiled cottages and gardens of Choumert Square, one of the most appealing sights on the walk.

Continue to a T-junction with Blenheim Grove, and turn right. A few yards before reaching Rye Lane turn left into the entrance to Peckham Rye station, and the end of Stage One of your walk. From Rye Lane there are regular bus services to Elephant and Castle, London Bridge, and various south London destinations.

Right: The next stage of the walk takes you through Stockwell, which possesses some fine houses, as this Georgian doorway in Clapham Road testifies

Stage Two: Peckham Rye to Clapham Common

Distance 6 miles. Intermediate distances: Southwark Town Hall 1 mile, Camberwell Station Road 2 miles, Loughborough Road 3 miles, Stockwell (Lansdowne Way) 4 miles, Larkhall Rise 5 miles.

Time 3-3½ hours.

Terrain All paved or tarmac paths, with one long, gradual stepped path at Wandsworth Road, easily avoided and described in the text.

Refreshments There is a choice of cafés and pubs in Peckham, Camberwell, Stockwell, and Clapham.

Toilets Rye Lane, Camberwell Green, Clapham. The toilets at Clapham Common station seem to be locked more often than not; a preferable option may be to patronize one of the many coffee shops or pubs around Old Town.

Transport Fare zone 2. Peckham Rye (train, bus), Camberwell Green (bus), Denmark Hill (train, bus), Stockwell (Tube, bus), Wandsworth Road (train, bus), Clapham Common (Tube, bus).

Best time to do the walk Monday to Saturday, when all the shops and cafés are open.

Left: The soaring spire of St Giles' Church, Camberwell is a local landmark

The ancient settlement of Peckham, in Old English 'peac' (hill), and 'ham' (village), 'the village by the hill', which at one time was crossed by two Roman roads, grew rapidly after the arrival of the Surrey Canal in 1826, the South Metropolitan gas works a few years later, and the establishment of many new businesses, such as Jones and Higgins huge department store. Prior to this great expansion the nearby village of Camberwell had the distinction of being the spot where the Camberwell Beauty butterfly was first seen in 1748. Sporting deep red wings, blue spots, and white edging, it now only occurs as a rare migrant from Scandinavia, so you probably won't see a live one here.

Start at Peckham Rye station in Rye Lane (trains from London Bridge, Victoria, Blackfriars, and West Croydon, buses from Elephant and Castle, London Bridge, Lewisham). **Turn left out of the station precinct, or from Rye Lane, into Holly Grove.** Follow a wide tarmac path that snakes its way through Holly Grove Shrubbery, with some of the original Victorian cottages to your left and right. **Turn right at the exit gate** from the shrubbery to continue along Holly Grove, crossing Bellenden Road.

At a T-junction with Lyndhurst Way keep on ahead to enter Warwick Gardens. Follow the path as it winds through this little park to Azenby Road, at the end of which **a left turn will take you along Lyndhurst Grove.** After 300 yards **turn right to follow Vestry Road.** Once you have passed a cluster of shops, **turn right through a gate into Lucas Gardens.** Carry on parallel with Vestry Road through the length of the gardens, passing under some mature trees, to **go through a gate onto Peckham Road,** with Southwark Town Hall opposite.

Apart from the Town Hall, there are several notable but contrasting buildings in this vicinity that are used for various council offices; to your right on Peckham Road is an elegant Georgian terrace, set well back from the road, and to the left the ultra-modern, functional Sunshine House.

Turn left to follow Peckham Road, pass Dagmar Road, and then **turn left into Wilson Road** at St Giles's Church.

Old St Giles's Church, which merited inclusion in the Domesday Book, was burnt to the ground in 1841, with the present building, with its soaring 210 ft spire, being erected by 1844. Inside the church there are a few brasses and relics rescued from the fire, while buried in the churchyard are said to be Agnes Skinner, who lived to 119; Mary, wife of John Wesley, the founder of Methodism; James Blake, who sailed with Captain Cook; and the Little Woman of Peckham, a schoolmistress who was just over two feet tall.

Walk along Wilson Road for 50 yards, then cross over and **turn right through a gate into the churchyard.** Take the middle one of three paths, to **go straight ahead through a gate and along brick-laid Churchyard Passage to Camberwell Grove,** with the Grove pub opposite.

Many of the houses here are part of the original 18th-and early 19th-century developments built on Camberwell's fields. At first Camberwell Grove just led to an old manor house, one of several in this vicinity where well-known families with names such as Bowyer and Champion de Crespigny had lived for generations.

Cross over Camberwell Grove, turn left, and after 50 yards turn right to follow an un-named passageway between house numbers 36 and 38. At the end cross Grove Lane and continue in the same direction, now on Love Walk. Follow this quiet backwater, passing Jennie Lee House and some secluded, tree-shaded cottages, to arrive at Denmark

Hill. **Turn right and walk to the traffic lights at Coldharbour Lane**. Cross to the left here, then turn right to cross Coldharbour Lane and continue towards Camberwell Green.

Dairy farming, market gardening, and fruit growing, all much in demand to supply the ever-expanding metropolis, occupied the villagers of Camberwell in pre-Victorian times. The village was noted for its fresh air and clean spring water, making the locality popular for those who could afford to 'commute'.

Camberwell Fair was a three-day annual event on the Green until stopped by local residents in 1855, by which time the presence of 'nomadic thieves, coarse men, and lewd women' required the services of twelve Bow Street Runners to keep order. Traffic is the problem nowadays, although even fifty years ago the Green was jammed with trams. The place would probably be unrecognisable to poet Robert Browning, born in Rainbow Cottage, Camberwell, in 1812, and writer John Ruskin, who both grew up here.

At Camberwell Green (there are toilets across the road, to the right), **turn left to follow Camberwell New Road.** Pass the bus garage, cross Camberwell Station Road, but **do not go under the bridge. Instead turn left,** then after 50 yards **turn right under another railway bridge to follow Knatchbull Road.** At a roundabout, make your way across the junction to **go ahead through a gate into Myatt's Fields Park.**

Strawberries and rhubarb were produced by Joseph Myatt in a market garden situated hereabouts, which occupied part of the large estate owned by the Minet family. This French Huguenot family began building on their land in the 19th century with houses of quality that still look good to this day. They also provided St James the Apostle Church, Longfield Hall, and the Minet Library, which used to be a much grander affair before being bombed in World War II. The park opened in 1889.

Keep left as you walk through the park, passing some fine old trees including a weeping ash and a knobbly old mulberry. **Leave the park by going through a gate** opposite the prominent spire of the former St James the Apostle Church, which has been converted by the Black Roof Housing Cooperative into 18 maisonettes. Now you are on Knatchbull Road again. **Turn right and carry on** past round-fronted Longfield Hall and the Minet Library.

At this point you cross Burton Road, where at number 80 former prime minister John Major lived with his parents. Just around the corner from there, at The Lodge in Akerman Road, music hall star Dan Leno was in residence around 1900.

At the next junction turn right to follow Lilford Road. Keep ahead across Akerman Road at a traffic light junction to continue past the few shops on Loughborough Road, and the grand old former Loughborough Hotel. **At Brixton Road cross over and turn right.**

Left: Streets of solid Victorian houses surround the former Loughborough Hotel

The Loughborough Hotel dates from 1900, which is

about the time that the Old White Horse, the building that was once a pub on the corner of Loughborough Road and Brixton Road, was rebuilt as you see it today. Both hostelries are having to adapt to a new way of life, and new uses, in the 21st century, while the worn and polished cobbles on the Brixton Road frontage of the old pub hark back to coaching days on this main route to Brighton. Beneath your feet at about this spot is the course of the River Effra, one of London's underground rivers, which flowed through Brixton to join the Thames at Vauxhall.

Continue north along Brixton Road for ¼ mile, **turn left into Hillyard Street and keep going to a junction with Hackford Road.**

Above: Vincent Van Gogh lived here – but not for long

Although your route is straight ahead, digress here for a moment by turning right for 20 yards to the first house in Hackford Road, number 87, which sports a blue plaque in honour of Vincent Van Gogh, who lived here from 1873–74.

Cross Hackford Road to Durand Gardens. Follow this road as it bends sharply right, and then continue along the right-hand pavement through this delightful oasis of Victorian living. **At Clapham Road turn left** for 120 yards, then **cross right at the lights to follow Lansdowne Way.** For Stockwell station simply continue on Clapham Road.

You may have noticed some of Stockwell's surviving Georgian buildings on Clapham Road. The old village green in Stockwell Road, and the site of the manor house nearby were obliterated by bricks and mortar long ago, but many fine old houses and points of interest are still to be found in the surrounding streets, some of which you now explore.

Press on along Lansdowne Way, crossing South Lambeth Road (with the cream-painted portico of Stockwell Baptist Church to your right), until you arrive at Stockwell bus garage.

Around 1950 four experimental designs for bus garages at Shepherd's Bush, Loughton, Thornton Heath, and this one at Stockwell were produced. Built between 1951–54, this concrete cathedral of transport has a 400 ft long parking area arched over with roof spans 194 ft long, reaching a height of 54 ft. The total area of over 73,000 sq ft can accommodate more than 200 buses. Statistics aside, the sheer utilitarian vastness of the place is most impressive, meriting English Heritage Grade II* listing.

At the Duke of Cambridge pub, turn right to follow Guildford Road. Take the first left, opposite the old church, into St Barnabas Villas, then **left again into Lansdowne Gardens,** a circle of handsome old dwellings.

Follow Lansdowne Gardens by turning left again, and continue to the end of this road, where the grand houses give way to a strange mixture of high-rise flats and rustic cottages. Now you make acquaintance with Lansdowne Way again. **Turn right for 100 yards, crossing to the left-hand pavement, then turn left at the Priory Arms** (well worth a visit for food, real ale, and an impressive collection of beer mats), and **follow Priory Grove.** Go along here for 130 yards, passing a go-kart track and a wooded adventure playground, then **turn right into Priory Mews,** through an arbour and seating area, to **enter Larkhall Park.**

Until it closed a few years ago, there used to be a local hostelry called the Larkhall Tavern. It had been named after a nearby mansion called Lark Hall, and now the name is kept alive in this green space. Larkhall Park was constructed in the 1970s from plans drawn up 30 years earlier, to provide more open space in this area of dense housing, much of which had suffered bomb damage in the Blitz.

Walk ahead along the park's perimeter,

Above: A tempting hostelry – The Surprise at Larkhall Park

passing a children's playground and then aiming slightly left for The Surprise pub in Southville, a short cul-de-sac. This homely little hostelry offers Young's ales, food, and outdoor seating right by the park. From the pub **walk the few yards to Wandsworth Road and turn left** (there are one or two more pubs and cafés here). Continue along Wandsworth Road for 50 yards and then **bear left across an open area at Courland Street,** this time taking the right-hand tarmac path across Larkhall Park. Pass another playground and a fenced-in sports pitch, at which you bear left to leave the park and then **turn right along Larkhall Lane.**

Above: Matrimony Place leads to the Eden Community Garden

Press on along long, straight Larkhall Lane, crossing Union Road (where Larkhall Lane becomes Larkhall Rise) and Albion Avenue, then **just before the railway bridge turn right to follow Killyon Road,** with Battersea Power Station's chimneys just coming into view (to avoid the steps in Matrimony Place, carry on over the bridge and keep on ahead to join up with the main route at Rectory Grove). **At Wandsworth Road turn left** to pass the railway station, then after a further 160 yards, by pedestrian lights, **turn left into Matrimony Place,** a stepped path which leads past the Eden Community Garden and St Paul's Church to emerge at Rectory Grove.

St Paul's occupies a site where there has been a church since the 13th century or earlier. The present building contains some fine monuments saved from the old church, including the late 17th-century Atkins monument, complete with Sir Richard and Lady Atkins and three of their children, all beautifully carved by William Stanton. The church you see now dates from 1815.

In 1837 the nearby moated manor house was demolished; it had been enlarged and rebuilt over the years, and with the church had been the nucleus of the old village of Clapham. Mansions and villas belonging to wealthy merchants and people of note encircled Clapham Common, but many of these were swallowed up in the rapid growth of the 18th and 19th centuries by builders such as Thomas Cubitt, developer of Pimlico and Belgravia, who built the Clapham Park estate. However, the next half-mile of your walk passes some of the oldest houses in the 'village', alongside many later styles of building.

With your back to the church go ahead to the road junction, then right, to follow Rectory Grove, passing Turret Grove (don't trouble yourself searching for a turret; this name refers to one, long gone, that topped one end of the old manor house). **At the roundabout junction with North Street, by the Old School, use the crossing to gain the left-hand pavement and continue in the same direction past the fine residences of Old Town.**

Below: An 18th-century house in Old Town, Clapham

Some of these houses date back to the days of Queen Anne; note the age-old railings at number 23, while opposite is Sycamore House of 1787, which for many years housed the Sycamore Laundry. A little further on, at number 43, there is a blue plaque recalling J F Bentley, architect of Westminster Cathedral, who lived in this handsome 300-year-old house. Later on in the walk you will see an example of his work at Corpus Christi Church, Brixton Hill. Across the road is The Polygon, originally built about 1790, with the jars above the corner shopfront, next to the Rose and Crown, reminding the passer-by that this was a grocer's shop until quite recently. Old Town is a good spot to stop for refreshment in one of the many pubs or cafés.

Carry on ahead as Old Town joins The Pavement, which curves round to the left to arrive at Clapham Common station.

Away to the right is Holy Trinity Church, built 1774–76 after an Act of Parliament was obtained enabling the church to be built on the common. Back on your side of the road the appetizing window displays of a top-notch delicatessen and patisserie are an invitation to treat yourself to something tasty, as you have now completed Stage Two of 'Village Life'.

Right: One of Clapham Old Town's tempting hostelries

Stage Three: Clapham to Brixton

Distance 2½ miles. Intermediate distance: Ashby Mill 1 mile.

Time 1½ -2 hours.

Terrain Step-free pavement and tarmac on the gentlest of slopes.

Refreshments Clapham's High Street and Old Town should cater for most tastes, while Brixton Station Road has a couple of cafés, with the market and surrounding streets offering Caribbean and other alternatives.

Toilets Clapham Common station (but see note on Stage Two), Brixton.

Transport Fare zone 2. Clapham Common (Tube, bus), Brixton (Tube, train, bus).

Best time to do the walk Monday to Saturday, to enjoy all the shops, cafés, and Brixton's lively streets and markets.

Left: Ashby Mill, which you will pass in Stage Three, eventually had to use steam and gas power as the surrounding buildings reduced the power of the wind

In Oliver Cromwell's time Clapham was known as a strongly Puritan village, mainly because the local gentry were that way inclined. The bewildered villagers had been told in 1644 that there would be no more 'wrestling, shooting, bowling, ... masques, wakes, otherwise called feasts, church ales, dancing, games, sports, or pastimes whatsoever. Maypoles to be taken down'. Life must have been deadly dull. Modern-day Clapham is quite the reverse; the common for recreation, shops, pubs, and restaurants to enjoy, and an 'upwardly mobile' population of young professionals from around the world.

Start at Clapham Common station, on the Northern line. **From the clock tower, with your back to the glass-domed station roof, cross right at the lights to turn right along Clapham Common South Side.** Continue past the parade of shops and the grand mansions of Crescent Grove, 60 yards after which you **turn left to follow Crescent Lane.** Following the lane's twists and turns, you will pass St Mary's School, and arrive at Abbeville Road. Cross straight over to continue along Crescent Lane.

At Park Hill keep on ahead, then cross King's Avenue at traffic lights, to a T-junction with Lyham Road. Turn right and then immediately left past a barrier, on a paved and concrete path beside a line of mostly empty shops. Pass another barrier and press on ahead, maintaining the same direction, through Ramillies Close, between modern low-rise housing with a shrubbery alongside. At the end of the planted area, you will arrive at an open space surrounded by a low, thick brick wall. **Turn right to follow a brick-laid path towards Windmill Gardens and Ashby Mill.**

The mill was built for John Ashby around 1816, and ground corn for the local farmers until encroaching buildings reduced the force of the wind, at which time it was converted to steam and then gas power. Ashby Mill was still grinding corn in 1924 according to a local guidebook, but ceased working ten years later. Look out for an old millstone lying in the grass nearby, and a glimpse of Brixton Prison further uphill, the original buildings of which date from 1820, just after the mill appeared on this hillside.

From Windmill Gardens keep on past another barrier and continue, now on Blenheim Gardens, to Brixton Hill, which you cross at the lights and then **turn left to carry on downhill**. Once across Brixton Water Lane **take the path half-right across Rush Common,** opposite the imposing edifice of Corpus Christi Catholic Church. Follow this tarmac path the full length of the common to **rejoin Brixton Hill, then continue your downhill route, across the busy junction with St Matthew's Road, and past St Matthew's Church.**

Rush Common is a wide strip of land alongside Brixton Hill, much of which was appropriated by Victorian house-builders to add the attraction of a long front garden, still evident at some of the older properties further up the hill. Lambeth Council is slowly restoring the common as a long-term project.

St Matthew's, here since 1824, was one of the 'Waterloo Churches', built to celebrate victory over France. It is Brixton's oldest church, with room for a congregation of 2,000, and in recent times has adapted to being not only a church but also a community venue. Faintly discernible on one of the gateposts is the instruction for 'Carriages to enter at this gate'.

Across the busy main road, displaying a tasteful Edwardian blend of brick and stone, is the impressive Lambeth Town Hall, dating from 1908.

From the central island just past the Budd family memorial cross right and carry on

Right: Sir Henry
Tate, a 'wise
philanthropist', in
front of the library
that he endowed

across Brixton Oval to the Tate Library. **Turn left to the Ritzy cinema.**

The bust of Sir Henry Tate, a resident of Streatham, in front of the library that he endowed recalls the man who benefited the nation by bringing us not only the Tate Gallery, but also the humble sugar cube. The inscription tells us that he was an 'upright merchant' and a 'wise philanthropist'.

Now the Village Life walk comes to a lively conclusion as you take a short tour through Brixton's market streets, with the opportunity to explore a labyrinth of indoor and outdoor stalls, selling just about everything under the sun. The original 'village' of Brixton, the name derived from 'Brixe's Stone', an ancient boundary marker of the Manor of Lambeth, had its origins on Brixton Hill.

A move downhill came once the railway opened up the area in the 1860s, when Brixton became a thriving town, with shops such as Bon Marche, one of the first ever department stores and eventually part of the John Lewis group, opening in 1877. In the 1880s Electric Avenue became one of the first streets to be lit by electricity, followed in 1911 by the opening of the Electric Pavilion, now the Ritzy Cinema, London's oldest cinema still used for its original purpose.

For many years the town centre maintained its position as one of south London's major shopping attractions, and although today the grandeur may have diminished somewhat, Brixton still has bags of verve and character.

Turn right at the cinema to follow Coldharbour Lane.

Above: Brixton's Ritzy cinema

Cross Electric Lane and Rushcroft Road, then at the traffic lights just before the railway bridge **turn left along Atlantic Road.** Market Row on the left and Brixton Village to the right are two well-patronized examples of the town's distinctive covered markets.

Left: Electric Avenue's well-stocked market

Just before a high railway viaduct crosses diagonally overhead, **turn right along Pope's Road,** where there are public toilets. **Go under a bridge and turn left along Brixton Station Road,** which offers two or three cafés, with the Recreation Centre on your right. **Carry on to the end of this road**, where you turn left on Brixton Road, then first left on Atlantic Road for 120 yards for trains to Victoria, Bromley South, and Orpington, or straight ahead for 100 yards to Brixton Underground station.

That's it; the end of your journey through a string of diverse and ancient settlements, all of which have changed dramatically since their days of rural isolation, but still maintain links with the past. Hopefully you have enjoyed this unique insight into south London life. Well done; now you can relax and immerse yourself in Brixton's exotic pleasures.

Right: One of several inviting entrances to the various covered markets in Brixton

10 Watermen's Woe

A Journey along the River Thames from Hammersmith to Tower Hill in four stages

This walk is a celebration of London's river and its crossings, providing an insight into the gradual change from the days of Old London Bridge, when the watermen, who ferried passengers up, down, or across the river, were an essential part of the city's prosperity. There were several thousand of them, carrying out a risky job which included perils such as 'shooting' through Old London Bridge's dangerously narrow arches, or falling victim to the press gang and ending up, unwillingly, at sea.

Eventually, privately funded toll bridges eclipsed the watermen's monopoly, but on this journey along the Thames tideway you may be able to capture some of the flavour of those far-off days while enjoying easy, toll-free, bridge crossings, each with its own unique viewpoint on the river.

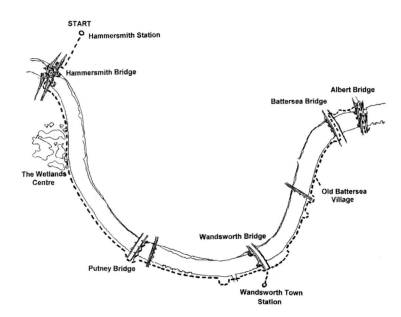

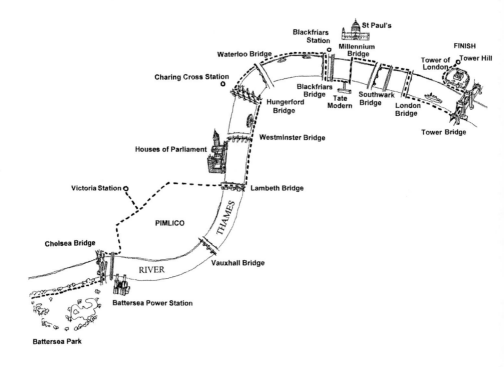

Stage One: Hammersmith to Wandsworth

Distance 4 miles. Intermediate distances: Barn Elms 1 mile, Putney Embankment 2 miles, Wandsworth Park 3 miles.

Time 2 hours.

Terrain Rough and sometimes muddy towpath from Hammersmith to Putney, otherwise fairly level paving and tarmac. Steps at Wandsworth Bridge easily avoided.

Refreshments Cafés and pubs in Hammersmith and Putney, a café in Wandsworth Park, and some choice in Old York Road, at walk's end.

Toilets Hammersmith Broadway, Putney, Wandsworth Park.

Transport Fare zones 2 & 3. Hammersmith (Tube, bus), Putney (train, bus), Putney Bridge (Tube, bus), Wandsworth Town (train, bus).

Best time to do the walk Anytime, but pick a day that's not too windy.

A s gyratory systems go, Hammersmith's is a busy one. Major routes radiate in every direction. But if you choose to cross the river here, you must use a charming, antique, but fragile structure to do it.

Start from the Broadway Shopping Centre, at Hammersmith Piccadilly and District line station (toilets here). **Follow signs for Apollo Theatre** (where there is an automatic toilet) and Riverside Studios. Pass to the right of the Apollo, and **continue along Queen Caroline Street to the riverside at Lower Mall; here turn right, then right again to gain the bridge,** by The Old City Arms pub. Cross the bridge, then go left down a ramp to the waterfront. Turn right, downstream, have a quick look back to admire the scene, and now let's get going. This first mile can be muddy in wet weather.

It was in 1827 that the first Hammersmith Bridge opened after the promoters overcame strong opposition from the owners of Putney and Kew bridges, jealous of any competition to their toll income. This practical but good-looking structure was quite a marvel at the time, being the first suspension bridge over the Thames, and its handsome stonework and white painted suspension chains could be admired at close quarters on payment of a halfpenny toll, taken by a liveried, top-hatted tollman.

Right: Hammersmith Bridge is an elegant reminder of a bygone age

With greatly increased traffic came the need for a new bridge, which was built to a design by Sir Joseph Bazalgette, Chief Engineer to the Metropolitan Board of Works. This was duly completed in 1887, but was immediately criticised for not being wide or strong enough. However, it's still with us today, having survived fractures, IRA bombs, nautical collisions and today's traffic levels.

In 1939, the bridge was saved from an Irish bomb plot by a hairdresser named Maurice Childs, who happened to be walking across the bridge at one o'clock in the morning and spotted two men who had stopped their car on the bridge. Investigating, he discovered a smoking suitcase, which he grabbed and flung into the river, where it exploded, sending a shoot of water as high as the bridge into the air. This brave man later received the George Cross.

Hammersmith Bridge enjoys these unique attributes; built-in seats, superb vistas up and down river, lots of rustic charm and a ring of coats of arms on the abutment casings, which are; clockwise from the horse (Kent) then Guildford, Westminster, Colchester, Middlesex, and the City of London. The Royal Arms are central.

As you cross the bridge, look for the tiny inspection doors on the towers, like something from Alice in Wonderland.

A tenuous link with the end of your walk occurs on the Barnes side, where the approach road was initially built up over marshy ground using spoil shipped up-river in barges from excavations for the new St Katharine's Docks, near Tower Hill.

Follow the riverbank towards Putney.

With fine views across the water, the luxury flats alongside reach a climax at Harrods imposing Depository buildings. As you progress, distant calls of wildfowl are evidence of the London Wetlands Centre, a unique bird reserve created here by Sir Peter Scott from the redundant Barn Elms reservoirs.

Look out for a memorial to Steve Fairbairn, famous oarsman, which marks the start of a scene of great sporting activity, with well-used playing fields to your right, oarsmen (and women) skimming enthusiastically up and down river, and Fulham Football Club's home at Craven Cottage over the water.

Soon a little bridge takes you across the outlet of Beverley Brook, a short but attractive Thames tributary. Rising in suburban Sutton and North Cheam, it has its own 6½ mile waymarked walk through some green and pleasant parts of Wimbledon Common, Richmond Park and Barnes.

Putney Embankment follows (automatic toilet here), with a backdrop of individual and interesting boathouses. On the opposite shore is tree-clad Bishop's Park, where hidden amongst the foliage is Fulham Palace, home of the bishops of London from the 11th century to 1973.

Back on your side of the river, a tempting hostelry comes into view. This is The Duke's Head, one of many Young's real-ale pubs in this vicinity. Brewed at Wandsworth since the 17th century until 2006, this tasty beer is now produced miles away in Bedford.

Left: There is usually plenty of rowing activity on Putney Embankment

Above: Historic St Mary's Church, Putney, is now a venue for orchestral concerts

Just before a slipway there is an unremarkable stone obelisk displaying the chiselled initials 'U B R' marking the University Boat Race start. A few yards further on, Waterman's Green, a rather forlorn little patch of vegetation on the bridge approach, is a rare memorial to those that spent their life on the river.

Do not cross Putney Bridge, instead **cross at the lights to St Mary's Church**. There is a café adjacent to the main building.

During the Civil War, this businesslike little church with its 15th-century tower was the scene of the 1647 Putney Debates, where calls for greater democracy and equality from officers within Oliver Cromwell's army, known as the 'Levellers', were too much for Cromwell, who was quick to re-assert his authoritarian regime. A plaque inside the church tells the story.

A few years later, in 1669, Samuel Pepys cheers us up with his account of a brief visit to this area; 'By water with my brother as high as Fulham, talking and singing, and playing the rogue with the Western bargemen about the women of Woolwich; which mads them.'

In spite of years of petitions and proposals, Putney had to wait until 1729 for its first bridge. It was made of wood, with 26 openings, and was straddled by a toll-house. At first called Fulham Bridge, for ½d a foot passenger could cross south to the fishing village, as it then was, of Putney, while persons of quality had to pay a shilling for their carriage and horses to cross when on a visit to one of the mansions on Putney Hill or at Roehampton. Old Putney Bridge was replaced in 1886 by the present elegant structure, again designed by Bazalgette.

From the church, follow a Thames Path sign, passing a war memorial cross, which takes you back to the riverside at the distinctive bulk of Putney Wharf. **Continue past the Boathouse pub** and a pavement café to **leave the river and**

emerge onto Deodar Road. Turn left here and continue to the end.

Originally built for the London and South-Western Railway, the iron-lattice bridge here carries the District line overhead, alongside which is a footbridge to Putney Bridge station. Deodar Road has the highly desirable, and unusual, asset of houses with gardens that lead right down to the riverbank.

Go straight ahead through Blade Mews into Wandsworth Park, and then follow the riverside row of noble London plane trees. At the far end of the park, near the playground, is a café, and there is an automatic toilet nearby in Putney Bridge Road.

Wandsworth Park's greenery is matched on the opposite bank by the exclusive Hurlingham Club, established in 1869 as a pigeon-shooting club, which occupies Hurlingham House, an 18th-century mansion, in a perfect setting. Over the years sports played here have included polo, tennis, cricket, golf, croquet, and archery, and the busy schedule continues to this day, but without the shooting, which ceased after a court case brought by a group of members in 1905.

Continue along the riverside, out of the park, and past some opulent houseboats. Immediately turn right into Point Pleasant, with the un-gentrified Cat's Back pub a possible refreshment stop. Just before a railway bridge, **turn left opposite**

Below: The Wandle joins the Thames at incongruously placed lights, just visible here at the mouth of the river

Prospect Cottages into Osiers Road. After the left-hand bend, **cross to follow Enterprise Way,** and keep ahead to cross the River Wandle.

Described as the hardest-worked river in the world, this fast-flowing watercourse rises in Waddon and Carshalton and then falls over 100 ft in its 9½ mile length. Thirteen watermills were recorded in the Domesday survey, and in later years over 90 mills were engaged in producing flour, snuff, oil, paper, copper, iron, and from 1881 included William Morris's famous printing works at Merton Abbey. One mill even produced, from wood, a red dye that was used to colour locally made hats for the clergy in Rome.

The Surrey Iron Railway, the first of its kind in the world, ran horse-drawn wagons from a riverside wharf here all the way to Merstham from 1803–48. Note the traffic lights, incongruously placed in the water at the mouth of the Wandle.

Continue ahead on Smugglers Way, passing the recycling areas. **Turn left on Waterside Path,** leading to Nickols Walk, where you rejoin the riverside briefly. Shortly before Wandsworth Bridge, the path takes you past the Ship pub, then ahead along Pier Terrace (or take the parallel road to avoid the steps). Steps at the end take you up to Wandsworth Bridge approach, where Stage One of your walk ends. For Wandsworth Town station, turn right, passing the bus stop and subway, to then cross the main road at pedestrian lights. Turn right and then left, through a small park, in company with a cycle track. The station is just under the bridge, in Old York Road.

That's the first section of 'Watermen's Woe' under your belt. Hopefully you have enjoyed it. The next stage is quite different; in fact each section has its own distinct character, so let's get going on Stage Two.

Stage Two: Wandsworth to Pimlico

Distance 4½ miles. Intermediate distances: Battersea Square 1 mile, Cheyne Walk 2 miles, Battersea Park Children's Zoo 3 miles.

Time 2½-3 hours.

Terrain There are a few steps on the riverside path, all of which can be easily avoided.

Refreshments Cafés in Battersea Square and Battersea Park, with Pimlico and Victoria offering every possible choice.

Toilets Battersea Park, Pimlico, Victoria.

Transport Fare zones 1 & 2. Wandsworth Town (train, bus), Battersea Bridge (bus) Battersea Park and Queenstown Road (train, bus), Victoria (Tube, train, bus), Vauxhall Bridge Road (bus).

Best time to do the walk
On a warm day, to enjoy a picnic in Battersea Park.

Left: Made in Coalbrookdale, Shropshire, this memorial commemorates the opening of Chelsea Embankment in 1874

Start at the southern end of Wandsworth Bridge, continuing from Stage One. (Wandsworth Town station, which is nearby, is served by trains from Clapham Junction.) An Act of Parliament sanctioning Wandsworth Bridge was passed in 1864, but design changes, indecision and disputes concerning approach roads meant spiralling costs, and when it finally opened in 1873, disappointing toll revenues added to the shareholders gloom. To cap it all, by 1880 the bridge tolls had been officially abolished. It was replaced by the present bridge in 1940.

On the bridge approach, **cross at the lights and continue along York Road,** with the colossal apartment blocks of Battersea Reach to your left. After ¼ mile, **turn left into Mendip Road.** At the end **turn right into Chatfield Road, then immediately left** up a brick ramp to the riverside, where **you turn right and continue alongside the Thames.** Sometimes there are cormorants drying their wings, phoenix-like, on an old jetty here.

Soon the walk leads past a car park and back to York Road. **Turn left here, and then left at the traffic lights to follow Lombard Road.** Pass the London Heliport, and then **follow the signed riverside walk.**

Here you pass the gigantic, curvaceous Falcon Wharf housing complex, next to a little old dock. Love them or loathe them, these giant Thameside developments have revolutionised access to the river, with their promoters being obliged to allow public enjoyment of the waterside. Two decades ago this walk would not have been possible. So here's a big thank you to all the pressure groups involved, which must have done a lot of arm-twisting on behalf of pedestrians.

You have to **divert briefly to go under Battersea Railway Bridge, then straight back to the waterside.** Just before St Mary's Church, turn right for 100 yards to Battersea Square, where you will find cafés, a pub, and shops. Take a few minutes to explore this historic village centre, then retrace your steps to the church, and continue along the riverside walk.

St Mary's Church stands proud, handsome, and alone next to the landing place that was the trading centre of old Battersea Village. It more than holds its own in eye-appeal compared to the high-rise, ultra-modern glass dwellings next door. On the opposite shore, Chelsea Harbour has the Belvedere high-rise block topped with a sliding ball that indicates the level of the tide. Next door to this exclusive development, Lots Road Power Station now stands idle, waiting for a new use.

Left: The riverside scene at St Mary's Church, Battersea

Right: Sir Thomas More sits in front of Chelsea Old Church

Soon you will arrive at Battersea Bridge. **Pass over the Thames to Cheyne Walk,** cross with care at the lights and **turn right.**

Old Battersea Bridge was opened in 1771. Financed by a consortium led by Earl Spencer, it was made of wood, with sixteen spans and a pronounced hump in the centre. It was one of the first London bridges to be lit, with oil lamps, then later with gas. This flimsy structure survived, with endless repair bills, until being replaced in 1890 by today's iron and granite Bazalgette-designed crossing. As you stroll over the bridge, look for the foundry name; 'Phoenix Iron Works, Derby'.

There is also a parish boundary marker set into the metalwork. At the bridge foot a statue of James McNeill Whistler, the famous artist who lived nearby, stands gazing over the river as if just about to capture some watery masterpiece.

Now you are in Chelsea, briefly, and along Cheyne Walk are some outstanding works of art, and buildings; on the corner of Danvers Street is Crosby Hall, rebuilt on this corner site in 1910, having been moved brick by brick from Bishopsgate in the City. The hall dates from 1466 and was originally just part of the palatial home of Sir John Crosby, soldier, alderman and wealthy businessman. This noble building housed many illustrious tenants over its long life in Bishopsgate, but in 1907 a City bank bought the freehold, and promptly announced plans to demolish the hall. Happily it was eventually saved, and reincarnated here.

Above: The artist Whistler surveys the scene at Battersea Bridge

Moving on, in the sunken, secluded Roper's Gardens is a beautiful nude statue entitled 'Awakening', and then in front of Chelsea Old Church is the compelling figure of Sir Thomas More, Lord Chancellor in Henry VIII's reign.

Within the churchyard is the tomb of Sir Hans Sloane, physician and one-time Lord of the Manor of Chelsea, whose name lives on in Sloane Square, Hans Crescent, and several other streets, while near to the racing riverside traffic is a green iron Coalbrookdale statue celebrating the 1874 opening of Chelsea Embankment, another engineering triumph of that familiar name, Sir Joseph Bazalgette.

In stark contrast to these illustrious citizens was Miser Neild, of number 5 Cheyne Walk, a landlord whose meanness extended to scrounging food from his hard-up tenants. He amassed a fortune of half a million pounds, which he left to Queen Victoria. She built Balmoral with it.

Follow Cheyne Walk to cross back to the riverside at the lights at Oakley Street, aiming for the green taxi driver's shelter, where you turn right and then left at another statue to **pass under Albert Bridge.**

Left: Albert Bridge is now fitted with a central prop

On the corner of Oakley Street is the charming 'Boy with a Dolphin', a statue that is full of movement and adventure, as if swimming full-pelt towards the stream.

Walk under the bridge, and then go left up steps to cross the bridge southwards, passing the redundant toll-booths, and the order for troops to break step when marching across.

It seems incredible that this fragile construction is still with us. Completed in 1873, the design, by RM Ordish, is an unusual cantilever and suspension combination. Hard-headed planners scheduled the bridge for replacement after the last war, but its good looks eventually won them over, and a central prop was fitted instead. Nobody could deny the appeal of

Albert Bridge, especially at night when lit and reflected in the moving waters beneath.

Once over the bridge, **go left through a gate into Battersea Park,** to regain the riverside walk, which will take you past the ornate, gilded, Buddhist Peace Pagoda. There are toilets by the Children's Zoo. **Continue by the river all the way to Chelsea Bridge,** which you walk under, and then immediately climb steps on the right (or use the lift) to gain the bridge. **Cross the river back to the northern shore.**

Battersea Park was at one time known as Battersea Fields, an area of some notoriety where cheap entertainment attracted undesirables; even an occasional duel was fought, the most famous being between the Duke of Wellington and Lord Winchilsea in 1829; the Duke deliberately missed, whereupon his opponent fired into the air. Respectability was restored when the park was laid out and opened in 1853, and nowadays the most striking feature of this pleasant 200-acre green oasis is the Buddhist Peace Pagoda, here since 1985. On the opposite shore is the Royal Hospital, home of the Chelsea Pensioners. In the river embankment at low tide you may be able to see the outfall of the Westbourne, which flows from Hampstead, then through a deep storm culvert under Hyde Park's green acres to eventually emerge here.

Below:
Ornamentation on
Chelsea Bridge

The first Chelsea Bridge was a government (as against privately) commissioned toll bridge. It was completed in 1858 at a cost of £95,000, a sum that was impossible to recoup in toll revenue. After just twenty-one years the bridge was declared toll-free, and in 1935 this ornamental old structure closed, to be replaced two years later by the present rather utilitarian crossing. The tower supports are interesting, being on hinged bearings.

Once you are over Chelsea Bridge, **cross Grosvenor Road at the lights and turn right.**

On your left is the former entrance to the long-lost Grosvenor Canal, which was well placed for transporting building materials during the development of Pimlico in the 1830s, and next door is the Western Pumping Station, quietly propelling millions of gallons of sewage on its way to be treated at Beckton, far away on London's eastern fringes. Trains rumble across Grosvenor Bridge on their way to and from Victoria station, while some of them stop for a rest in the sidings close by.

Go under the railway bridge, glance across the river at the stark outline of Battersea Power Station, and **take the first left into Lupus Street. Go left again after 50 yards into Turpentine Lane**, which you follow to its end.

Ahead of you as you turn off Lupus Street is Peabody Avenue, a private estate that has a strange feeling of Victorian austerity about it. Your route, however, takes you along canyon-like Turpentine Lane, which skirts round the back of these sombre dwellings.

On joining Sutherland Street, **continue in the same direction to a roundabout junction**

with Warwick Way, where you turn right. Follow this road, crossing Belgrave Road and St George's Drive to arrive at a cluster of shops.

This is Pimlico, a sizeable area of well-built Victorian dwellings just to the south of Belgravia. Both districts were developed by Thomas Cubitt, a prolific London builder, whose statue can be seen at the southern end of St George's Drive. Pimlico is a bit of a backwater, but a very pleasant one, with lots of individual shops (butcher, baker, etc.) a market in Tachbrook Street (where there are toilets, 40 yards down on the left), and enough eating and drinking venues to satisfy all tastes. It's also a perfect place to end Stage Two of your walk, with Victoria station close at hand, and plentiful bus services, from Victoria and Vauxhall Bridge Road.

Left: Battersea Power Station is the subject of major redevelopment plans

For Victoria station, turn left up Wilton Road, or for buses on Vauxhall Bridge Road continue ahead on Warwick Way, which is also the start of Stage Three.

Right: You will pass Victoria Tower Gardens, a pleasant spot for a break, in Stage Three

Stage Three: Pimlico to Blackfriars

Distance 3½ miles. Intermediate distances: Lambeth Bridge 1 mile, Hungerford Bridge 2 miles, Temple 3 miles.

Time 2½ hours.

Terrain Straightforward paving and tarmac all the way, with lifts at Hungerford Bridge.

Refreshments Victoria, Pimlico, and Horseferry Road offer numerous possibilities. There is a riverside tea bar near Lambeth Palace, and plenty of places around Charing Cross and Villiers Street. Victoria Embankment Gardens has a café, there is a pub at Temple station, and New Bridge Street, Blackfriars, has some choice.

Toilets Victoria, Pimlico, Old County Hall, near Embankment station.

Transport Fare zone 1. Victoria (Tube, train, bus), Vauxhall Bridge Road (bus), Pimlico (Tube, bus), Waterloo (Tube, train, bus), Charing Cross (Tube, train, bus), Embankment (Tube, bus), Temple (Tube, bus), Blackfriars (Tube, train, bus).

Best time to do the walk

On a day when you don't need to rush, as there is a lot to see on this section.

Left: Sir Arthur Sullivan in Embankment Gardens

Vauxhall is the one bridge you do not see on this walk, due to your inland detour to sample the pleasures of Pimlico. However, the bridge and its environs are interesting, and can be found mentioned in the 'Wilkes and Liberty!' walk.

Start in Warwick Way, at its junction with Wilton Road, continuing from Stage Two (If you are starting from Victoria station, follow signs for Station Reception, which will lead you to Exit 2, Wilton Road. There are toilets here, on Platform 1. Turn right to follow Wilton Road for ¼ mile to traffic lights at Warwick Way, where you turn left to start the walk). From Warwick Way, **cross Vauxhall Bridge Road to follow Rochester Row, directly opposite. Take the first right into Walcott Street, then left at Vincent Square.**

You may see some sporting activity in the centre of the square, where Westminster School have their playing fields. The Royal Horticultural Society's Old Hall is on the north-east side of the square.

Follow the square round to the right, then take the second left turn into Maunsel Street, which you follow to the end. There are more toilets here. Cross the end of Regency Street (Regency Place) to **continue in the same direction, now on Horseferry Road. At the roundabout junction with Millbank, use the zebra crossings to get to the left-hand pavement of Lambeth Bridge, which you cross.**

For centuries, there was a horse-ferry operating at the spot where Lambeth Bridge now stands, with the toll revenues going to the Archbishop of Canterbury at Lambeth Palace. In 1708 a man and horse would have to pay 2d to cross, while for a coach and six you would have to fork out 2/6d. An early form of drive-on, drive-off vessel, it once sank under the weight of Archbishop Laud's worldly goods, thankfully with the loss of just one carriage. A suspension bridge designed by PW Barlow was the first structure to be erected here, in 1862, to replace the ferry. Rather cheaply built, it proved troublesome and by 1910 was demoted to being a footbridge only. Its replacement, which you are crossing, was opened in 1932 and feels solid and dependable, with good old-fashioned riven paving slabs.

Once on the Lambeth shore, **turn left to follow Albert Embankment.** To your right is Lambeth Palace, and a little further on are the old and new buildings of St Thomas's Hospital. This is a fine spot to appreciate the elaborate design of the Houses of Parliament opposite. At Westminster Bridge, ignore the steps, and **carry on underneath the bridge.**

Glance up as you emerge, to see the rear end of the South Bank Lion that stands on the parapet. Originally adorning the nearby Red Lion Brewery, now long gone, it is an example of Mrs Coade's waterproof artificial stone, the secret of which was lost with the factory's closure in 1840.

Old Westminster Bridge was a handsome structure, but with poor foundations. Opened in 1750, it saved long detours to either Putney or London bridges, which were the only alternatives, apart from the horse-ferry. The bridge you see today replaced the earlier one in 1862, having been designed to harmonise with the Houses of Parliament and the Embankment.

Now you pass the former County Hall and The London Eye. There are toilets in the main building here, next to the café. **Keep on along the riverbank to climb steps (or use the lift) to the Golden Jubilee Bridge, which you cross** (this is the Hungerford Bridge, one either side of the railway line. You can use either one)

These dual footbridges are a convenience and a delight. Masking the businesslike steelwork of Charing Cross's railway approach, they replace an earlier footway tacked onto the railway bridge. This in turn had taken the place of Brunel's original Hungerford footbridge, opened in 1845 to provide access to Hungerford Market at Charing Cross. Ten thousand people a day paid their tolls to use this first bridge, making it an instant success, but within two decades the South-Eastern Railway muscled in, demolished all but the piers, and threw their own uncompromising structure across the river. The chains of Brunel's bridge survived, being used on the Clifton Suspension Bridge near Bristol.

Once on the Charing Cross side, **carry on downstream on Victoria Embankment**, passing Embankment station. There are toilets just past the station. **Go through a gate into Victoria Embankment Gardens,** and turn right to follow the path between flower beds and statues.

This is a perfect spot to pause and refresh, with nearby Villiers Street and the gardens themselves having reasonably priced cafés; soon after leaving this green oasis you will be entering the City of London, whose riverside walkways are somewhat lacking in home comforts.

Over to the left is the 17th-century stone Watergate, all that remains of York House; this was the home of George Villiers, first Duke of Buckingham. While allowing his land to be developed, he insisted his full title must be used in the names of the streets created here, hence at the top of Villiers Street is York Place, formerly 'Of Alley'.

Memorials to the great and good are plentiful here, and include a most poignant tribute to Arthur Sullivan;

> 'Is life a boon?
> If so, it must befal
> That death, when'er he call
> Must call too soon'. W.S.Gilbert

He gazes serenely out from his plinth-top, unaware of the abject female admirer below. On the Embankment, opposite the end of Northumberland Avenue, is a modest wall plaque to Sir Joseph Bazalgette, 1819–91, chief engineer to the Metropolitan Board of Works, and the driving force behind the construction of London's river embankments, sewerage system and several Thames bridges.

The gardens finally peter out at Savoy Street, where you **continue ahead, passing under Waterloo Bridge.**

John Rennie was the architect of the original Waterloo Bridge, which was completed in 1817. Even then, the bridge with its approach roads cost over £1m, but was said to be the most beautiful of London's bridges. Italian sculptor Antonio Canova said it was; 'the noblest bridge in the world, alone worth coming to London to see'. It must have been good, but with vastly increased traffic levels by the 1920s a dip had developed on the Strand side. Whether to repair or replace caused bitter arguments for years, and Herbert Morrison, the London County Council's leader, showed his feelings by performing an impromptu demolition ceremony, throwing a few loose bricks into the river. No doubt he was delighted to be able, eventually, to open this graceful new bridge in 1944, to the design of Sir Giles Gilbert Scott.

Now you walk alongside the rusticated arches and pillars of Somerset House. Originally designed as a palace for the Duke of Somerset, it was still incomplete by the time of his execution in 1552. To provide stone and clear the building site, the Duke had demolished a church, several houses, and an Inn of Chancery. Overstepping the mark, his workmen arrived at St Margaret's, Westminster to grab more stone, only to be repulsed by club and bow wielding parishioners. Later residents included Queen Elizabeth I and Charles II's Queen, Catherine of Braganza. In 1775, the old palace was demolished and, over several years, Somerset House re-emerged as you see it now. Just think how grand this river frontage must have looked when there was no Embankment, and no traffic, except on the water.

Keep on along the Victoria Embankment, crossing Temple Place, where an imposing statue of I K Brunel, without his familiar stovepipe hat, stands on a corner site. Pass Temple Gardens to eventually meet Middle Temple Lane on your left.

Here is the Temple, headquarters of the Knights Templar in the 12th century until their fall from grace in the 1300s. At that time the lawyers started moving in, and they are still there today. Fixed to the railings you will see the emblems of Pegasus (Inner Temple) and Lamb and Flag (Middle Temple). You now leave the City of Westminster, and passing two fearsome dragons, enter the City of London.

Below: One of the dragons at Inner Temple that guard the City of London's boundary

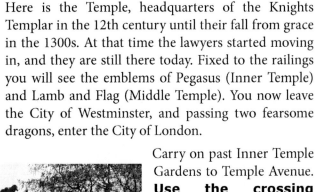

Carry on past Inner Temple Gardens to Temple Avenue. **Use the crossing here to regain the riverbank.** Follow the pavement down a ramp and under Blackfriars Bridge, then climb steps to go up to the bridge (to avoid the steps, cross the bridge at the pedestrian crossing). Stage Three ends here. For Blackfriars train and Tube stations, turn away from the river and continue past the drinking fountain, to the subway and station entrances.

Stage Four: Blackfriars to Tower Hill

Distance 3 miles. Intermediate distances: Millennium Bridge/ St Paul's 1 mile, HMS Belfast 2 miles.

Time 2 hours.

Terrain Ingenuity and a little map-reading are required to avoid several flights of steps on this section.

Refreshments Coffee bars and pub at Blackfriars, cafés at Tate Modern. In the City, St Paul's Crypt café (and toilets) is only ¼ mile off route, while Bow Lane and Garlick Hill, which are near Mansion House station, are good places to stop. Further on, Cannon Street, London Bridge, and Tower Hill all have something to offer.

Toilets Tate Modern at Bankside, St Paul's Cathedral and Paternoster Square, Suffolk Lane/ Upper Thames Street (near Cannon Street station), Eastcheap (near The Monument), More London Place (opposite H M S Belfast), Tower Hill (behind Group Tickets Office and Welcome Centre).

Transport Fare zone 1. Blackfriars (Tube, train, bus), Mansion House (Tube, bus), Cannon Street (Tube, train, bus), Monument (Tube, bus), London Bridge (Tube, train, bus), Tower Hill (Tube, bus), Tower Gateway (DLR), Fenchurch Street (train).

Best time to do the walk Try to avoid the crush of tourists at holiday times.

Left: The Millennium Bridge provides a direct link between Tate Modern and St Paul's

Above: Blackfriars Bridge was widened in 1907–09 to provide tramways

Named after the 13th-century monastery of the Black Friars, the first bridge here opened in 1769. The Gordon rioters of 1780 took exception to paying a toll of ½d, and burnt down the toll-house. Like so many of London's bridges it suffered from 'scour' caused by an increased flow of water after the removal of the barrier-like structure of Old London Bridge and was replaced in 1869 with the present bridge, by Joseph Cubitt. Looking north from the bridge the valley of the Fleet River follows New Bridge Street and Farringdon Road to pass under Holborn Viaduct on the way to its source in Hampstead. Once it was a waterway wide enough for ships to enter, but now it can only be seen issuing from a little arch by the bridge at low tide.

Start from Blackfriars station by crossing Blackfriars Bridge. Once over the bridge, descend steps to the riverside pavement and **go under Blackfriars Railway Bridge** towards the Tate Modern.

A handsome, but now decapitated, relic of the 1860s railway boom, this first bridge was designed with the road bridge to ensure that the piers did not hinder river traffic. The first train crossed in 1864, twenty years before the second bridge was erected.

Continue past the Founders Arms pub to arrive at Tate Modern (café and toilets here), where you ascend a ramp to **cross the Millennium Bridge, towards St Paul's.**

Nicknamed 'The Wobbly Bridge' because of an alarming swaying (since rectified with dampers) this pleasing structure would have been a hit in the days of toll charges. Tourists love it, as it provides a handy link between the grandeur of St Paul's and the Tate's dramatic bulk. Whoever dreamed up the idea of a footbridge here deserves a medal.

At the foot of the bridge, turn right down steps (or use the lift) to Paul's Walk, where you continue your eastward journey through various twists and turns, **following Riverside Walk East signs.** These will lead you away from the waterside to join High Timber Street. Pass Stew Lane to **turn right at Queenhithe,** opposite a metal footbridge, back to the water's edge. If this access is closed, carry on for 50 yards, turning right at Kennet Wharf Lane to regain the riverbank.

Viewed across the water, there are three eye-catching buildings; the former Bankside Power Station sporting its 325 ft chimney, the rebuilt Globe Theatre, and Riverside House, looking somewhat like a huge, shining onion. At the side of this ultra-modern block, in Bear Gardens, is an ancient relic; a ferryman's seat, of unknown date, let into the wall, and remote from the passing riverside hordes.

As you arrive at Southwark Bridge, go left into Fruiterers Passage. Depictions of various stages of bridge construction line this tiled pedestrian route under the roadway.

John Rennie designed the first bridge here, which opened in 1819. Nearly 6,000 tons of cast iron went into this massive undertaking, but it was not a success, being only 28 ft wide. Over a century passed before the present wider bridge was erected, but it still has a forgotten air about it. Only one bus route uses this bridge; even in the days of trams, things were much the same.

Continue along Three Cranes Walk, passing a waste transfer station at Walbrook Wharf. Your route now goes through a concrete-strengthened arched way **under Cannon Street railway approach to Allhallows Lane, then past rows of seats on Waterman's Walk** (turn left here for automatic toilet on the other side of Upper Thames

Street, slightly to the left). Carry on **under London Bridge** (seven steps to climb here), and cross a little bridge over 'stairs' going down to the river. **After Adelaide House (the first office block) turn left to St Magnus the Martyr Church.**

Try to picture the tumult here when the footway to the old bridge went straight through the porch. Church opening times are (usually) Tuesday-Friday 10:00-16:00, Sunday 10:00-13:00. If you get the chance, do go in, for apart from an unexpectedly sumptuous interior, there is on display an impressive model of Old London Bridge, true to detail, showing the daily ebb and flow of human and animal traffic amongst the houses and shops that lined both sides.

Above: At one time, the footway to London Bridge passed through the porch of St Magnus the Martyr Church

From the porch turn left to go just under the bridge, where you will immediately see on your left a passage which, via steps, emerges onto London Bridge. Go ahead to **cross the bridge.**

Amazingly, until the great era of 18th-and 19th-century bridge-building, London possessed but one permanent structure straddling the Thames, and that was Old London Bridge. This famous, revered, ancient crossing was narrow and congested, so that between the diverse ranges of buildings that lined both sides of the bridge was squeezed much of the cross-river traffic of an expanding city, be it wheeled, hoofed, or on foot.

There had already been a crossing here for nearly one thousand years when King Olaf of Norway famously destroyed part of the bridge while attacking the Danish stronghold of London. That was in 1014, after which various wooden structures were built, destroyed by fire or flood and then rebuilt. Around 1176 Peter de Colechurch, a builder-priest, began the first stone bridge, which was soon augmented with houses, shops, a chapel, drawbridge and gatehouse which, located at the Southwark end, frightened visitors with a gruesome display of traitor's heads on poles.

The bridge provided a defence for the City, but a barrier to the river. 'Shooting' the bridge, trying to navigate a boat through the strong currents of one of the nineteen arches, was sometimes a fatal gamble. So restricted was the flow of water that a particularly harsh winter could result in a frozen river, which the citizens took advantage of by holding 'frost fairs' on the ice, with the most famous fair of 1683 featuring horse-racing, bull-baiting, and booths selling all manner of goods. An enterprising printer set up his press, producing souvenir leaflets printed in the middle of the frozen river.

London Bridge became so clogged that in 1722 three traffic controllers were appointed, with for the first time instructions to keep traffic to the left, and to prevent disorderly conduct and delays while the tolls were being collected.

By 1762, all the buildings on the bridge had been demolished in an effort to modernise and protect the now crumbling structure. Incredibly, this ancient monument was still in use until an elegant replacement, designed by John Rennie, was opened in 1831. This later bridge has ended its days as a tourist attraction in Arizona, having been sold, in 1968, to the McCulloch Oil Corporation for nearly 2.5 million dollars.

New London Bridge is sleek, stylish, well-designed and easy on the eye, and blends with the high-rise City skyline. But as you stride across, look 100 yards downstream and picture, if you can, the medieval bustle, noise and pageant of Old London Bridge. It must have been quite a sight.

Right: City Hall
provides a base for
the Mayor of London

Once across, at No 1 London Bridge, **descend awkwardly angled steps to The Queen's Walk,** which you follow all the way to Tower Bridge.

Progress along here can be slow due to your eyes being drawn to the towers and spires of the City opposite, where Old Billingsgate Market and the Custom House front an ever-growing, awe-inspiring conglomeration of corporate wealth-creation. As you pass World War II survivor HMS Belfast (turn right for automatic toilets, some way down by the shops) and the strange lopsided blob of City Hall, the Tower of London and Tower Bridge fill your view.

This bridge is a youngster compared to Old London Bridge, having been opened in 1894. Its stone-clad steel towers are so well known as to prompt one American tourist, queuing on the bridge to visit the 'Tower Bridge Experience' to ask 'is this the Tower of London?' Perhaps she can be forgiven, for it was planned to blend in, using granite and Portland stone, with the historic scene. Sadly the City Architect, Sir Horace Jones, did not live to see his project through to completion. Sir John Wolfe Barry and a third-generation Brunel, Henry Marc, were the engineers.

Arriving at Tower Bridge, climb steps on the left to then cross the bridge. At the last arch, central pavement steps lead down, under the roadway. On emerging here, **turn left back under the bridge in front of the Tower,** passing Traitor's Gate. **At Tower Pier go right, uphill.** There are toilets located on the left behind the Welcome Centre and Group Tickets building. For Tube, DLR, and buses continue uphill (cross at the pedestrian lights here to avoid most of the steps), then right, to soon turn left under the roadway, and up steps.

Above: Tower Bridge was designed to harmonise with the Tower of London

Your long riverside ramble ends here, on Tower Hill, next to the Tower of London. Built by William the Conqueror to subdue and overawe the restless Londoners, the Tower has been fortress, palace, and prison over its 900 year life, and now it packs in the tourists. What a momentous place this is to end your walk. On the way you will have briefly visited seven London Boroughs, the Cities of Westminster and London, and travelled over, under, or across twenty-one bridges; foot, rail and road. Best of all, you will have viewed the capital from its prime vantage point; the river. Why not have a celebratory drink, and rest your weary feet.

Contacts

Alexandra Palace 020 8365 2121 www.alexandrapalace.com

Apsley House 020 7499 5676 www.english-heritage.org.uk

Bank of England Museum 020 7601 5545 www.bankofengland.co.uk/museum

Banqueting House 0844 482 7777 www.hrp.org.uk

Brent Reservoir (Welsh Harp) www.waterscape.com

British Museum 020 7323 8299/8000 www.thebritishmuseum.ac.uk

Brunel Museum 020 7231 3840 www.brunel-museum.org.uk

Buckingham Palace www.royal.gov.uk

Camden Lock 020 7485 7963 www.camdenlockmarket.com

Charterhouse tours to book call 020 7251 5002

Church Farmhouse Museum 020 8359 3941 www.churchfarmhousemuseum.co.uk

Churchill Museum and Cabinet War Rooms 020 7930 6961 www.iwm.org.uk

City of Westminster www.westminster.gov.uk

City of London Information Centre 020 7332 1456 www.cityoflondon.gov.uk

Clapham www.clapham/society.com

Clink Prison Museum 020 7378 1558 www.clink.co.uk

Cuming Museum 020 7525 2332 www. southwark.gov.uk/cumingmuseum

Deptford www.deptford.towntalk.co.uk

Florence Nightingale Museum 020 7620 0374 www.florence-nightingale.co.uk

Friends of the City Churches 020 7626 1555 www. london-city-churches.org.uk

Gabriel's Wharf, Oxo Tower 020 7021 1600 www.coinstreet.org

Golden Hinde 08700 11 8700 www.goldenhinde.org

Green Flag Awards (Parks) www.greenflagaward.org.uk

Hackney Museum 020 8356 3500 www.hackney.gov.uk/museum

Hampstead Heath www.cityoflondon.gov.uk/openspaces

Highgate Cemetery 020 8340 1834 www.highgate-cemetery.org

Holland Park www.rbkc.gov.uk

Houses of Parliament www.parliament.uk

Imperial War Museum 020 7416 5320 www.iwm.org.uk

Kensington Palace 0844 482 7777 www.hrp.org.uk

Lee Valley Park 01992 702200 www.leevalleypark.org.uk

London Boroughs www.london.gov.uk

London Canal Museum 020 7713 0836 www.canalmuseum.org.uk

London Fire Brigade Museum 020 8555 1200 x39894 www.london-fire.gov.uk

Market information www.eastlondonmarkets.com

Museum of Garden History 020 7401 8865 www.museumgardenhistory.org

Open House London 020 3006 7008 www.openhouse.org.uk

Pumphouse and Rotherhithe Heritage Museum 020 7231 2976 www.thepumphouse.org.uk

Regent's and Grand Union Canals 020 7985 7200 www.waterscape.com

River Thames www.riverthames.co.uk

Roundhouse 0844 482 8008 www.roundhouse.org.uk

Royal Parks www.royalparks.org.uk

St John's Gate Museum 020 7324 4005 www.sja.org.uk/museum

Somerset House 020 7845 4600 www.somerset-house.org.uk

Southwark Cathedral 020 7367 6700 www.southwark.anglican.org/cathedral

Southwark Visitor Information www.visitsouthwark.com

Tate Modern 020 7887 8888 www.tate.org.uk/modern

Tower Bridge Exhibition 020 7403 3761 www.towerbridge.org.uk

Tower of London 0844 482 7777 www.hrp.org.uk

Vestry House Museum 020 8509 1917 www.lbwf.gov.uk

Wellington Arch 020 7930 2726 www.english-heritage.org.uk

Westminster Abbey 020 7222 5152 www.westminster-abbey.org

William Morris Gallery 020 8527 3782 www.lbwf.gov.uk/wmg

Bibliography

These are some of the books on London that have been extremely helpful:

Anderson, Sarah & Davies, Miranda. *Inside Notting Hill,* Portobello Publishing, 2001

Barton, Nicholas. *The Lost Rivers of London,* Historical Publications, 1998

Beasley, John D. *The Story of Peckham and Nunhead,* London Borough of Southwark, 1999

Boast, Mary. *The Stories of Camberwell, Walworth, Bermondsey and The Borough* (4 Volumes), London Borough of Southwark, 1993–2000

Cosh, Mary. *An Historical Walk through Clerkenwell,* Islington Archaeology and History Society, 1987

Essex-Lopresti, Michael. *Exploring the New River,* Brewin Books, 1997

Fiddes, Angela. *The City of London,* Pevensey Press, 1984

Gay, Ken. *A Walk around Muswell Hill,* Hornsey Historical Society, 1987

Hailstone, Charles. *Hammersmith Bridge,* Fulham and Hammersmith Historical Society, 1987

Harwood, Elain & Saint, Andrew. *London,* HMSO, 1991

Humphrey, Stephen. *The Story of Rotherhithe,* London Borough of Southwark, 1997

Jackson, Alan. *London's Local Railways,* David & Charles, 1978

Kent, William & Thompson, Godfrey. *An Encyclopaedia of London,* JM Dent, 1970

Mathewson, Andrew & Laval, Derek. *Brunel's Tunnel,* Brunel Exhibition, Rotherhithe 1992

Morris, Simon & Mason, Towyn. *Gateway to the City,* Hornsey Historical Society, 2000

Nicolson, Jim. *Vauxhall Gardens 1661-1859,* The Vauxhall Society, 1991

Pepys, Samuel. *Diary 1659-1669,* Frederick Warne, 1933

Pevsner, Nikolaus. *The Buildings of England; London, Except the Cities of London and Westminster,* Penguin, 1952

Pevsner, Nikolaus & Bradley, Simon. *The Buildings of England; London 1: The City of London,* Yale University Press, 2002 *London 6: Westminster,* Yale University Press, 2003

Pinching, Albert. *Discovering Old Wood Green,* Hornsey Historical Society, 1998

Piper, Alan. *Brixton Heritage Trails,* The Brixton Society, 2001

Pudney, John. *Crossing London's River,* J M Dent, 1972

Rankin, Stuart. *Rotherhithe History Walks,* Southwark Local History Library, 2004, 2005

Richardson, John. *Camden Town and Primrose Hill Past,* Historical Publications, 1991

Shields, Pamela. *Essential Islington,* Sutton Publishing, 2000

Shute, Nerina. *London Villages,* Robert Hale, 1977

Shute, Nerina. *More London Villages,* Robert Hale, 1981

Schwitzer, Joan. *Highgate Walks,* Hornsey Historical Society, 2004

Snow, Len. *Willesden Past,* Phillimore, 1994

Tucker, Tony. *The Visitor's Guide to the City of London Churches,* 2006

Valentine, K J. *Neasden: A Historical Study,* Charles Skilton, 1989

Weinreb, Ben & Hibbert, Christopher. *The London Encyclopaedia,* Macmillan, 1993

Williams, Harry. *South London,* Robert Hale, 1949

Index

Albert Bridge 240
Albert Memorial 46
Alexandra Palace 169
Apsley House 42
Archway Bridge 178
Ashby Mill 223

Bank of England 13
Bankside 21,120
Banqueting House 83
Barnsbury 93
Barry, Charles 82
Battersea Bridge 238
Battersea Park 241
Battersea Square 238
Battle of Waterloo 78
Bazalgette, Sir Joseph 230, 248
Bermondsey 128
Beverley Brook 232
Black Eagle Brewery 115
Black Prince 79
Blackfriars Bridge 251
Blackfriars Road 23
Blow-up Bridge 190
Blue, The 128
Borough High Street 124
Borough Market 121
Boundary Street Estate 114
Brent Reservoir (Welsh Harp)
  162
Brick Lane 115
British Museum 87
Britton Street 74
Brixton 224
Broadway Market 112
Brock's Fireworks 210
Brunel Museum 139
Brunswick Centre 88
Buckingham Palace 40

Caledonian Market 94
Caledonian Park 93
Camberwell Green 215
Camberwell Grove 214
Camden Lock 95
Camden Mews 94

Canada Water132
Chalk Farm 188
Charterhouse 70
Chelsea Bridge 241
Cheyne Walk 239
Christ Church, Spitalfields 116
Church Farmhouse Museum
  164
Churchill Museum 36
City Churches 15-21
City of London 10-21
Clapham 219
Clapton Square 107
Clerkenwell 72
Clerkenwell Green 73
Clink Prison Museum 122
Cockpit Steps 36
Columbia Road Market 114
Cool Oak Bridge 162
Cornhill 14
Corporation of London 172
County Hall 27
Cowcross Street 74
Crocker's Folly 192
Cromwell, Oliver 44
Crosby Hall 239
Cuming Museum 126

Deptford 202
Deptford Creek 205
Deptford Town Hall 207
Diana, Princess of Wales 48
Dickens, Charles 22, 125
Dollis Hill 157
Dollis Hill WW2 Command
  Bunker 158
Doulton's Pottery 80
Dudding Hill Junction 156

Elephant and Castle 126
Ely Place 68
Embankment Gardens 247

Farringdon Station 74
Fetter Lane 67
Florence Nightingale Museum

  27
Frestonia 146

Gabriel's Wharf 63
George Inn 123
Gibbons, Grinling 204
Girdlers' Company 210
Gladstone Park 157
Gladstone, William 157
Golden Hinde 122
Goldsmith's College 207
Gordon Riots 67, 82
Grand Surrey Canal 132
Grand Union Canal 148, 195
Green Park 41
Greenland Dock 132
Grosvenor Canal 242
Gwynne, Nell 182

Haberdashers' Company 208
Hackney 108
Hackney Empire 110
Hackney Museum 111
Haggerston Park 113
Hammersmith Bridge 230
Harlesden 151
Hatcham 208
Hatton Garden 68
Hendon 163
Hendon Aerodrome 164
Hendon Fair 163
Hick's Hall 71
Highgate Cemetery 180
Highgate Village 176
Highgate Wood 173
Highpoint 174
Hippodrome Place 145
Holland House 50
Holland Park 49
Holy Trinity Church, Clapham
  221
Hop Exchange 122
Hornsey Historical Society
  177
Horse Guards Parade 37
Household Cavalry Museum

37
Houses of Parliament 82
Hungerford Bridge 246
Hurlingham Club 234
Hyde Park 44
Hyde Park Corner 42

Imperial War Museum 59
Islington Tunnel 92

Johnson, Dr Samuel 64
Jones, Sir Horace 68, 255

Kensington Gardens 46
Kensington High Street 48
Kensington Palace 47
Keystone Crescent 92
King Charles I 83
King Charles II 37
King George III 48, 54
King Henry VIII 26, 70
King William III 47
King's Cross 89, 92

Lambeth Bridge 56, 245
Lambeth Palace 81
Lambeth Walk 59
Larkhall Park 218
Lee Valley Regional Park 105
Little Venice 193
Livery Companies 19
London Bridge 253
London Canal Museum 92
London Central Meat Market 68
London Fields 111
London Fire Brigade Museum 23
London Necropolis Station 25
London Stone 18
Long Water 45
Lost rivers
Effra 57,217
Fleet 251
Neckinger 141
Tyburn 41
Walbrook 17
Westbourne 241
Lower Marsh 25
Ludgate 66

Maida Hill Tunnel 192
Mansion House 15

Markets 97-117,206
Marshalsea Prison 125
Metropolitan Railway 161
Metropolitan Tabernacle 126
MI6 Building 57
Middlesex Sessions House 73
Millbank 55
Millennium Bridge 251
Mitre Tavern 68
Museum of Garden History 81
Muswell Hill 171
Myatt's Fields 215

Nash, John 178,191
Neasden 161
Nelson Dock 135
New Cross Gate 207
Notting Hill 199
Nunhead 210
Nunhead Cemetery 209

Of Alley 247
Old Oak Lane 149
Old Vic Theatre 24
Oxo Tower 63

Parkland Walk 171
Parliament Hill 184
Parliament Square 29
Parnell House 87
Peasant's Revolt 81
Peckham Rye 210
Pepys, Samuel 206, 233
Peter Pan statue 46
Peter the Great 205
Petticoat Lane 117
Pimlico 243
Portobello Road 197
Potteries 144
Primrose Hill 189
Prince Henry's Room 66
Prince Lee Boo 139
Pumphouse Museum 136
Putney Bridge 233

Queen Anne's Gate 36
Queen Caroline 46
Queen Elizabeth I 31
Queen Victoria Memorial 39

Regent's Canal 112, 190
Rennie, John 248, 252
Rivers

Brent 158,163
Lea 105
New River 168
Ravensbourne 202
Thames 228-256
Wandle 235
Rotherhithe 135
Rotherhithe Tunnel 138
Round Chapel 106
Roundhouse 188
Roundwood Park 152
Royal Courts of Justice 64
Royal Exchange 12
Royal Parks 36-46
Rush Common 224
Russell Square 88
Russia Dock Woodland 133

Serpentine 45
Seven Dials 86
Sloane, Sir Hans 239
Smithfield 68
Somerset House 63, 248
South Bank Lion 27, 246
Southwark 118
Southwark Bridge 22, 252
Southwark Cathedral 121
Southwark Park 129
Spitalfields Market 116
Spring Gardens 78
St Andrew's Church, Kingsbury 162
St Bartholomew the Great Church, Smithfield 69
St Clement Danes Church 64
St Dunstan in the West Church, Fleet Street 66
St Etheldreda's Chapel 68
St George the Martyr Church, Borough 124
St George's Circus 60
St Giles 87
St Giles's Church, Camberwell 214
St James's Church, Clerkenwell 73
St James's Palace 38
St James's Park 36
St John's Gate 71
St John's Square 72
St John-at-Hackney Church 107
St Leonard's Church,

Shoreditch 114
St Magnus-the-Martyr
  Church, London Bridge 253
St Margaret's Church,
  Westminster 29
St Mary Abbots Church,
  Kensington 48
St Mary's Church, Battersea
  238
St Mary's Church, Hendon 164
St Mary's Church, Putney 233
St Mary's Church, Rotherhithe
  139
St Mary's Church,
  Walthamstow 101
St Mary-le-Strand Church 64
St Matthew's Church, Brixton
  224
St Nicholas' Church, Deptford
  204
St Pancras 89
St Paul's Church, Clapham 219
St Paul's Church, Deptford 203
St Peter's Church, Walworth
  127
St Saviour's Dock 141
St Thomas's Hospital 25
Stave Hill 137
Stockwell 217
Stockwell bus garage 218
Strand 64
Surrey Commercial Docks
  132-7
Surrey Quays 130
Sutton House 108

Tate Britain 56
Tate, Sir Henry 56, 225
Telegraph Hill Park 208
Temple 249
Temple Bar 65
Theatreland 86
Tooley Street 141
Tower Bridge 255
Tower of London 256
Trafalgar Square 84
Trellick Tower 196
Trinity Church Square 125

Van Gogh, Vincent 217
Vauxhall 57, 78
Vauxhall Bridge 56
Vauxhall City Farm 58

Vauxhall Iron Works 80
Vestry House Museum 100
Victoria Embankment
  Gardens 247
Victoria Tower Gardens 55, 82

Walbrook 16
Walthamstow Market 102
Walthamstow Marsh 104
Walthamstow Village 100
Wandsworth Bridge 237
Wandsworth Park 234
War memorials 37, 42
Waterloo 61
Waterloo Bridge 63, 248
Waterlow Park 179
Wellington Arch 41
Westminster 29, 54, 83
Westminster Abbey 30
Westminster Bridge 27, 246
Westminster Hall 29, 83
Westway 146
Whitehall Palace 83
Whittington, Dick 20, 179
Wilkes, John 52
Willesden Green 154
Willesden Junction 151
William Morris Gallery 102
Winchester Palace 122
Witanhurst 183
Wren, Sir Christopher 17
Wrestlers Tavern 174
Wood Green 168
Wormwood Scrubs 147

About the Author

Patrick Hamilton has lived and worked in London since 1965, after being raised in a part of rural Berkshire where walking was a daily necessity.

Throughout the 1980s and 90s England's long-distance paths were the focus of his weekend expeditions, and in recent years the discovery of London's history has happily combined with the pleasure of exploring the capital on foot.

Liking nothing better than the chance to investigate and learn about another corner of this great city, he is now devising new routes for the next instalment of *Walking Across London*.